THREE PLAYS

Mario Vargas Llosa lives in Lima, Peru. He is a novelist of international standing whose works include: *Aunt Julia and the Scriptwriter*, *The Real Life of Alejandro Mayta*, *The War of the End of the World*, *Who Killed Palomino Molero?*, *The Perpetual Orgy* and *The Storyteller*.

by the same author

AUNT JULIA AND THE SCRIPTWRITER
THE REAL LIFE OF ALEJANDRO MAYTA
THE WAR OF THE END OF THE WORLD
CAPTAIN PANTOJA AND THE SPECIAL SERVICE
THE PERPETUAL ORGY
WHO KILLED PALOMINO MOLERO?
THE STORYTELLER

MARIO
VARGAS LLOSA

THREE PLAYS

The Young Lady from Tacna
Kathie and the Hippopotamus
La Chunga

Translated by
DAVID GRAHAM-YOUNG

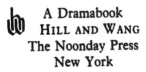

A Dramabook
HILL AND WANG
The Noonday Press
New York

www.fsgbooks.com

P 1

CONTENTS

The Young Lady from Tacna 1

Kathie and the Hippopotamus 77

La Chunga 155

ACKNOWLEDGEMENTS

I would like to thank everyone who helped me with these translations, especially Mario Vargas Llosa, Marilyn Watts, and the actors who took part in the rehearsed readings at the Gate Theatre.

D. R. G.-Y.

THE YOUNG LADY FROM TACNA

A Play in Two Acts

To Blanca Varela

INTRODUCTION

Lies that tell the truth

Although generally one might say that *The Young Lady from Tacna* explores such themes as old age, pride, and individual destiny, there is one underlying and pervasive idea encompassing all the others, which has turned out to be, I believe, the backbone of this play: it is the question of how and why stories come into being. I don't mean how and why they are written, for although Belisario is a writer, literature is only one area of the vast field of story-telling, present in every culture, including those that have no written language.

It is as fundamental an activity for the individual as it is for societies as a whole – it is in fact an essential part of human existence, a means of enduring the burden of life. But why does man need to tell stories? Why does he need to be told them? Perhaps because, through helping him contend with death and failure, as it did Mamaé, it gives him an illusory sense of permanence and relief. It is a means of retrieving, through a system controlled by the memory with the help of the imagination, a past that, when it was actually being lived, had all the appearance of chaos. Story-telling, fiction, thrives on what real life – in all its bewildering complexity and unpredictability – inevitably lacks: a sense of order, of coherence, of perspective, a period of time in isolation in which a hierarchy of facts and events can be determined, the relative importance of the characters, causes and effects, and the links between the actions. In order to understand what we are, as individuals and as nations, our only recourse is to come out of ourselves, and, with the help of memory and imagination, throw ourselves into the world of fiction in which we are portrayed paradoxically as something similar to, yet different from, what we really are. Fiction is the 'complete' man, a perfect blend of truth and falsehood.

Stories are seldom faithful to what they appear to be relating, at least in any quantitive sense: the word, whether spoken or written, is an entity in itself and distorts what it is supposedly

5

trying to communicate. Memory is deceptive, selective and partial. The gaps it leaves, which are generally not accidental, are filled by the imagination: every story therefore has some elements added to it. These are never arbitrary or fortuitous, because they are governed by that strange force which is not the logic of reason but that of dark unreason. Creativity is often little more than a form of retaliation against a life we find hard to live: we perfect it, or debase it in accordance with our own cravings and feelings of bitterness; we rework the original experience, modify what actually happened in order to satisfy the demands of our frustrated desires, our broken dreams, our feelings of joy or anger. In this way, the art of telling lies, which is the art of story-telling, is also, surprisingly, the art of communicating a deep-seated hidden truth about humanity. An imperceptible mixture of authentic and concocted events, of real and imaginary experiences, story-telling is one of the few forms – perhaps the only one – capable of depicting man in his entirety, both in his everyday life and in his fantasies, as he is and as he would like to be.

'The criterion of truth is to have invented it oneself,' wrote Giambattista Vico, who maintained, in an age when scientific cant was rife, that man was only really capable of understanding what he himself created: that is to say, the history of humanity rather than the physical world of nature and the universe. I don't know if that is true or not, but his principle is a marvellous vindication of the truth in story-telling, the truth in literature. This truth doesn't lie in any similarity or slavish adherence of the spoken or written word (what is created) to a higher 'objective' reality, but in itself, as something created from the raw material of truth and falsehood which make up the ambiguous totality of human experience.

I've always been fascinated by that strange process: the birth of a work of fiction. I've been writing now for quite a number of years, and it has never ceased to intrigue and surprise me, that slippery and unpredictable path, along which the mind travels, as it probes memories, calling up the most secret desires, impulses, whims, in order to 'invent' a story. While I was writing this play, I was sure I was going to re-create (taking

6

quite a few liberties on the way) the story of a familiar character, who was connected with my childhood, but I never suspected that under this pretext I was in fact attempting to tell the story of that elusive, transitory, changeable yet eternal process through which stories themselves come into being.

Mario Vargas Llosa

CHARACTERS

MAMAE, an old lady of about a hundred

GRANDMOTHER CARMEN, her cousin, somewhat younger and better preserved

GRANDFATHER PEDRO, Carmen's husband

AGUSTIN, their elder son, in his fifties

CESAR, their other son, somewhat younger than his brother

AMELIA, their daughter, younger than César, and in her forties

BELISARIO, Amelia's son

JOAQUIN, a Chilean officer, young, handsome and dapper

SEÑORA CARLOTA, elegant and beautiful, in her thirties

SET AND COSTUME

The stage is divided into two sets: the grandparents' house in Lima during the 1950s, and Belisario's study, which can be anywhere in the world in 1980. The majority of the action takes place in the grandparents' house: the living room cum dining room of a modest middle-class flat. There are two doors, one leading on to the street, the other to the inner part of the house. The furniture reflects the family's financial straits, which are verging on the desperate. The essential pieces of furniture are the old armchair where Mamaé has spent the best part of her latter years, the little wooden chair, which she uses as a walking aid, an old wireless set, and the table where the family supper takes place in Act Two. There is a window on to the street, through which trams can be heard going past.

The set should not be realistic. It is as Belisario remembers it. It is a figment of his imagination and so objects and characters should take on a reality separate from their real-life counterparts. Besides, in the course of the action, the same set is used to represent various different locations: a drawing room in the house in Tacna where Grandmother and Mamaé lived when they were young; the dining room of the house in Arequipa, when Grandfather was managing the Camaná cotton plantation in the twenties; the house in Bolivia where Mamaé told Belisario stories during the 1940s, and Pedro's lodgings in Camaná where he wrote his wife the letter Mamaé read in secret. The set has also to represent locations that are purely imaginary, such as Padre Venancio's confessional. So it is appropriate for it to have a certain indeterminate quality which facilitates (or at any rate doesn't hinder) these transformations.

Belisario's study consists of a plain wooden table covered in papers, notebooks, pencils, and perhaps a portable typewriter. However simple it is, it is important that it should reflect a man whose life revolves round his writing, who spends most of his time there; it is the place where, apart from writing, sleeping and eating, he delves into his past life, confronts himself with it and speaks to his phantoms. Belisario may be between forty

9

and fifty, or even older. Either way, he has had considerable experience as a writer, and what happens to him in the course of this story will almost certainly have happened to him on previous occasions. Judging by his clothes and general appearance, he is a man without resources, disorganized and careless.

The dividing line between the two different sets may be apparent or not as required by the production.

The costumes should perhaps be realistic, as one method of signalling the time changes from one scene to another could be in the way the characters dress. The Chilean Officer should wear a uniform from the beginning of the century, with gold buttons, belt and sword, and Señora Carlota a dress of the same period. The grandparents and Mamaé should dress modestly in clothes that place them firmly in the 1950s. As for Belisario, he is a character of today and his clothes, hair, etc., should reflect this.

This translation of *The Young Lady from Tacna* was first performed as a rehearsed reading on 8 April 1989 at the Gate Theatre, Notting Hill. The cast was as follows:

MAMAE	Sheila Grant
BELISARIO	Geoffrey Collins
GRANDFATHER PEDRO	John Burgess
GRANDMOTHER CARMEN	Diana Bishop
SEÑORA CARLOTA	Anna Gilbert
JOAQUIN	Alan Barker
AMELIA	Anna Gilbert
CESAR	Colin Bruce
AGUSTIN	William Haden
Director	David Graham-Young

ACT ONE

The stage is in darkness. A voice can be heard. It is MAMAE. *She sounds anxious, distressed and agitated. The lights come up, revealing that unforgettable face of hers: a mass of wrinkles.*

MAMAE: The rivers, the rivers are overflowing . . . Water, little
  drops of water, foam, everything's being drenched by the
  rain, it's coming in waves, the whole world's being
  swamped, it's the flood, the waters are seeping through,
  they're bursting out, escaping everywhere. Cataracts are
  forming, bubbling, it's the deluge, little drops of water,
  the river . . . Ahhh!
  (Lights come up on the whole stage. MAMAE *is sitting huddled
  in her old armchair and there is a little puddle at her feet.*
  BELISARIO *is at his desk, writing furiously. His eyes are lit
  up, and as he writes, his lips move as if he were dictating
  something to himself.)*
AMELIA: *(Coming in)* Oh, for heaven's sake Mamaé, you haven't
  peed again on the sitting-room floor already, have you?
  Why don't you ever ask? Then at least we could take you
  to the bathroom. The amount of times you've been told.
  I suppose you think I enjoy it? Well, I'm fed up with you
  and your filthy habits! *(Sniffs.)* I hope you haven't done
  something else as well.
  (A gesture of irritation from AMELIA *which* MAMAE *responds
  to with a smile and a little bow. She falls asleep almost
  immediately.* AMELIA *mops up the mess with a cloth. As*
  AMELIA *has been talking,* BELISARIO's *attention has
  gradually been wandering, as if his mind has been taken off
  his writing by some sudden extraneous idea. He puts his pencil
  down. He looks discouraged. He talks to himself, in a mumble
  to begin with.)*
BELISARIO: What are you doing here, Mamaé, in the middle
  of a love story? A little old woman who used to wet and
  dirty her knickers, who had to be put to bed, dressed,
  undressed and cleaned up, because her hands and feet no
  longer did what she wanted them to do – what can a person

like that be doing in a love story? (*Hurls his pencil on the floor in a sudden fit of anger.*) Well, are you going to write a love story or what, Belisario? Am I going to write something or what? (*Laughs at himself, becomes depressed.*) It's always worst at the beginning, it's the most difficult part of all, when all those doubts and feelings of inadequacy are at their most crippling. (*Looks at* MAMAE.) Every time I start something new, I feel like you, Mamaé, I feel like an old man of eighty, or a hundred, and my thoughts dart about like grasshoppers, just like yours did, when you were that complicated, helpless little creature we all laughed at, felt sorry for and were even a little afraid of. (*Gets up, goes over towards* MAMAE *and slowly walks round her, with the pencil he has picked up from the floor between his lips.*) But your mind was still a hive of activity, wasn't it? Had you lost your teeth by then? Of course you had. And you couldn't wear those false ones Uncle Agustín and Uncle César gave you because they scratched your gums. What on earth are you doing here? Who invited you? Don't you realize you're stopping me from working? (*Smiles and returns to his desk, spurred on by a new idea.*) Mamaé . . . Mamaé . . . Didn't somebody once call you Elvira? No, it wasn't Grandma, or Grandpa, or Mama, or my uncles either. (*Sits at his desk and starts to write on the sheets of paper in front of him, slowly at first, then becoming more fluent.*) The name sounded so strange to people outside the family. 'Why do you call her that? What does it mean, where did it originate?' Yet they all ended up calling her Mamaé too.
(*Exit* AMELIA, *who has finished cleaning the floor. As* BELISARIO *reaches the end of his speech,* JOAQUIN, *the Chilean officer, comes in. His uniform is of the style worn at the turn of the century; it is brightly coloured with silver or gold braid.* BELISARIO *will carry on writing throughout the whole of the following scene; he spends most of his time absorbed in his papers, but pauses occasionally, putting the end of his pencil to his mouth and chewing it, as some new idea comes to him or he recalls some incident from the past. By way*

14

of light relief, he turns round at odd moments to watch MAMAE
and JOAQUIN, *and takes a passing interest in what they say.*
Then he returns to his papers to write or read over what he
has written. The expression on his face is constantly changing.)

JOAQUIN: (*Whispering, as if leaning over a wrought-iron grille or*
balcony) Elvira . . . Elvira . . . Elvira . . .
(MAMAE *opens her eyes. She listens; smiles mischievously and*
looks around; she is flustered and excited. Her movements and
speech are now those of a young woman.)

MAMAE: Joaquín! But he's out of his mind. At this hour! Uncle
and Aunt are going to hear him.

JOAQUIN: I know you're there, I know you can hear me. Come
out, just for a second, Elvira. I've got something
important to say to you. You know what it is, don't you?
You're beautiful, I love you, and I want you. I can hardly
wait till Sunday – I'm literally counting the hours.
(MAMAE *sits up. Although clearly delighted, she remains*
demure and reticent. She goes over to the wrought-iron grille.)

MAMAE: Whatever do you mean by coming here at this hour,
Joaquín? Didn't anyone see you? You're going to ruin my
reputation. Here in Tacna the walls have ears.

JOAQUIN: (*voraciously kissing* MAMAE's *hands*) I was already in
bed, my love. When suddenly I had this feeling, right
here in my breast; it was like an order from a general,
which I had to obey: 'If you hurry, you'll find her still
awake,' it seemed to say. 'Make haste, fly to her house.'
It's true, Elvira. I had to see you. And touch you.
(*He eagerly tries to grasp her round the waist, but she shies*
away from him.)
If I hadn't been able to see you, I wouldn't have slept a
wink all night . . .

MAMAE: But we spent all afternoon together, Joaquín! What a
lovely walk we had in the garden with my cousin! When
I heard you, I was just thinking about all those
pomegranates and pear trees, quinces and peaches. And
the river, wasn't it looking lovely too? How I'd like to go
plunging into the Caplina again sometime, just as I used
to when I was a little girl.

JOAQUIN: This summer, if we're still in Tacna, I'll take you to the Caplina. We'll go at night. When no one will see us. To that same pool we had tea at this afternoon. We'll take off all our clothes . . .

MAMAE: Oh hush, Joaquín, don't start . . . !

JOAQUIN: . . . and bathe together naked. We'll play in the water. I'll chase you and when I catch you . . .

MAMAE: Please, Joaquín! Don't be so uncouth.

JOAQUIN: But we're getting married on Sunday.

MAMAE: I won't have you being discourteous to me when I'm your wife either.

JOAQUIN: But I respect you more than anything in the world, Elvira. I even respect you more than my uniform. And you know what a uniform means to a soldier, don't you? Look, I couldn't be discourteous to you, even if I wanted to. I'm making you annoyed, I know. I do it deliberately. Because I like it when you're like this.

MAMAE: When I'm like what?

JOAQUIN: You're such a sensitive little flower. Everything seems to shock you, you're so easily intimidated, and you blush at the least provocation.

MAMAE: Isn't that how well-brought-up young women should behave?

JOAQUIN: Of course it is, Elvira, my love. You can't imagine how I ache for Sunday. The thought of having you all to myself, without any chaperons. To know that you depend on me for the slightest thing. What fun I'm going to have with you when we're alone together: I'll sit you on my knee and make you scratch me in the dark like a little kitten. Oh, and I'll win that bet. I'll count every hair on your head; there'll be more than five thousand, you'll see.

MAMAE: Are you going to count them on our wedding night?

JOAQUIN: Not on our wedding night, no. Do you want to know what I'm going to do to you on our wedding night?

MAMAE: (*Covering her ears*) No! No, I don't!

(*They laugh.* MAMAE *mellows.*)

Will you be as loving and affectionate as this after we're married, I wonder? You know what Carmencita said to

16

me on our way back from the walk: 'You've really come up trumps with Joaquín, you know. He's good-looking, well-mannered, in fact quite the little gentleman in every way.'

JOAQUIN: Is that what you think too? You mean you don't mind that I'm a Chilean any more? And you've got used to the idea of being one yourself?

MAMAE: No, I have not. I'm a Peruvian, and that's the way I'm going to stay. I'll never forgive those loathsome bullies who won the war. Not till the day I die.

JOAQUIN: It's going to be very funny, you know. I mean, when you're my wife, and I'm posted to the garrison in Santiago or Antofagasta, are you going to spend all day arguing with my fellow officers about the War of the Pacific? Because if you say things like that about the Chileans, you'll get me court-martialled for high treason.

MAMAE: I'd never jeopardize your career, Joaquín. Whatever I think of the Chileans, I'll keep it strictly to myself. I'll smile and make eyes at your fellow officers.

JOAQUIN: That's enough of that! There'll be no smiling or making eyes at anybody. Don't you know I'm as jealous as a Turk? Well, with you, I'm going to be even worse.

MAMAE: You must go now. If my aunt and uncle found you here, they'd be so upset.

JOAQUIN: Your aunt and uncle. They've been the bane of our engagement.

MAMAE: Don't say that, not even in fun. Where would I be now if it hadn't been for Uncle Menelao and Aunt Amelia? I'd have been put in the orphanage in Tarapacá Street. Yes, along with all the bats.

JOAQUIN: I know how good they've been to you. And I'm glad they brought you up like some rare exotic bird. But we have been engaged for a whole year now and I've hardly been alone with you once! All right, I know, you're getting anxious. I'm on my way.

MAMAE: Till tomorrow then, Joaquín. At the eight o'clock Mass in the Cathedral, same as usual?

JOAQUIN: Yes, same as usual. Oh, I was forgetting. Here's that book you lent me. I tried to read Federico Barreto's poems, but I couldn't keep my eyes open. You read them for me, when you're tucked up snug in your little bed.

MAMAE: (*Pulling out a hair from her head and offering it to him*) I'll whisper them in your ear one day – then you'll like them. I'm glad I'm marrying you, Joaquín.

(*Before he leaves,* JOAQUIN *tries to kiss her on the mouth, but she turns her face away and offers him her cheek. As she goes back towards her armchair, she gradually takes on the characteristics of an old woman again.*)

(*Looking at the book of poetry*) What would Joaquín do, I wonder, if he knew about the fan? He'd challenge the poor man to a duel – he'd kill him. You'll have to destroy that fan, Elvira, it's just not right for you to keep it.

(*She curls up in her armchair and immediately falls asleep.* BELISARIO *has looked up from his papers. He now seems very encouraged.*)

BELISARIO: That's a love story too, Belisario. Of course, of course. How could you be so stupid, so naïve? You can't set a love story in an age when girls make love before their first Communion and boys prefer marijuana to women. But Tacna, after the War of the Pacific – when the city was still occupied by the Chilean Army: it's the perfect setting for a romantic story. (*Looks at* MAMAE.) You were an unrepentant little chauvinist then, weren't you Mamaé? Tell me, what was the happiest day in the life of the young lady from Tacna?

MAMAE: (*Opening her eyes*) The day Tacna became part of Peru again, my little one!

(*She crosses herself, thanking God for such bounteous good fortune, and goes back to sleep again.*)

BELISARIO: (*Wistfully*) It's one of those romantic stories that don't seem to happen any more. People no longer believe in them – yet you used to be so fond of them, didn't you, old friend? What do you want to write a love story for anyway? For that meagre sense of satisfaction that doesn't really seem to compensate for anything at all? Are you going to put yourself through all that agonizing humiliation

yet again, Belisario, just for that? Yes, you are – for that
very reason. To hell with critical conscience! Get away
from here, you damned spoilsport! Bugger your critical
conscience, Belisario! It's only good for making you feel
constipated, impotent, and frustrated. Get out of here,
critical conscience! Get out, you filthy whore, you tyrant
queen of constipated writers.
(*He gets up and runs over to where* MAMAE *is sitting. Without
waking her up, he kisses her on the forehead.*)
Welcome back, Mamaé. Forget what I said to you, I'm
sorry. Of course, I can use you. You're just what I need
– a woman like you. You're perfectly capable of being the
subject of a beautiful and moving love story. Your life
has all the right ingredients, at least to be going on with.
(*Returning to his desk*) The mother dies giving birth to
her, and the father not long after, when she was only . . .
(*Looks at* MAMAE) How old were you when my great-
grandparents took you in, Mamaé? Five, six? Had
Grandmother Carmen been born yet?
(*He has sat down at his desk; he holds the pencil in his hands;
he talks slowly, trying to find the appropriate words so he can
start writing.*)
The family was very prosperous at the time, they could
afford to take in homeless little girls. They were
landowners, of course.

MAMAE: (*Opening her eyes and addressing a little boy she imagines
is sitting at her feet*) Your great-grandfather Menelao was
one of those gentlemen who carried a silver-knobbed cane
and wore a watch and chain. He couldn't stand dirt. The
first thing he did when he went into someone's house was
to run his finger over the furniture to see if there was any
dust. He only drank water or wine out of rock crystal
goblets. 'It makes all the difference to the taste,' I
remember him saying to us. One evening he went out to
a dance with Aunt Amelia all dressed up in white tie and
tails; he caught sight of your grandmother Carmen and me
eating some quince preserve. 'Aren't you girls going to
offer me a bite?' he said. As he was tasting it, a little drop

fell on his tailcoat. He stood there staring at the stain.
Then, without saying a word, without causing any fuss, he
emptied out the whole pot of preserve and smeared it all
over his shirt front, tailcoat and trousers. Your great-
grandmother used to say: 'To Menelao, cleanliness is a
disease.'

(*She smiles and falls asleep again. During her speech,*
BELISARIO *has been listening part of the time to what she's
been saying, but he has also been jotting down notes and
reflecting.*)

BELISARIO: Your great-grandfather Menelao must have been
fascinating, Belisario. Yes, a fascinating old bastard. He'll
do, he'll do. (*Looking up at heaven*) You'll do, you'll do.
You and Amelia my great-grandmother adored Mamaé.
You brought her up as your own daughter, treating her
exactly the same as Grandmother Carmen, and when she
was going to get married to the Chilean officer, you sent
away to Europe for the wedding dress and trousseau. Was
it Paris? Madrid? London? Where did they order your
wedding dress from, Mamaé? Where was the most
fashionable place? (*Writes frantically.*) I like it, Belisario, I
love you, Belisario. I'm going to give you a kiss on the
forehead, Belisario. (*His mind wanders.*) How rich the
family was then! It's been on the decline ever since,
sliding further and further down the ladder until it finally
got to you! One setback after another! (*Looks up at
heaven.*) Whoever told you to marry an infantry captain,
Mama? But I'm not in the least bit sorry about your
misfortune, Papa. You've got to be pretty stupid to play
Russian roulette just after you're married! And you've got
to be even stupider to go and kill yourself in the process!
You've got to be pretty daft not to remarry when you're
widowed so young, Mama! Why did you pin so much hope
on me? How did you all get it into your heads that by
winning lawsuits I'd somehow bring fame and fortune back
to the family?

(*His voice fades in to the sound of a radio play which*
GRANDMOTHER *is trying to listen to; she is sitting in the*

20

*living room with her ear glued to the wireless. The announcer
is telling us that the daily episode of a radio serial by Pedro
Camacho has just finished. The noise of a tram is heard outside.*
MAMAE *opens her eyes, excited.* BELISARIO *watches her from
his desk.*)

MAMAE: Carmen! Carmen! Here it comes! Quick! Come over
to the window! Look, the Arica train!

GRANDMOTHER: (*Stops listening to the wireless and looks at*
MAMAE, *saddened yet amused*) I envy you, Mamaé, I really
do. You've found the perfect means of escaping from all
this misery that surrounds us. I'd like to go back to my
childhood too, even if it were only in a dream.

MAMAE: Aaah! My eyes! I could tear them out! I can't even
guess what anything is any more. Can you see that? Is it
the Arica train? Or is it the one from Locumba?

GRANDMOTHER: Neither. It's the Chorrillos tram. And we're
not in Tacna, we're in Lima. You're not a fifteen-year-
old girl any more, Elvira, you're a doddery old woman of
ninety, or thereabouts. And you're going gaga.

MAMAE: Do you remember the fancy-dress ball?

GRANDMOTHER: Which one? I went to lots of fancy-dress balls
when I was a girl.

MAMAE: At the Choral Society. You remember, the one the
negro sneaked in on.
(*The sound of a party can be heard; people enjoying themselves
– rhythmic dance music. Gradually the tune of an old-
fashioned waltz starts to predominate.*)

GRANDMOTHER: Ah, that one. Of course, I remember. It was
at that dance I met Pedro. He'd come from Arequipa to
spend carnival in Tacna, with some friends. Who'd have
thought I'd marry him! Yes, of course. Was that the time
Federico Barreto wrote that poem on your fan? No, it
wasn't, was it? It was one of those 28th of July affairs at
the Patriotic Ladies' Society. The negro, you're quite
right . . . It was you he was dancing with when they
discovered him, wasn't it?
(BELISARIO *gets to his feet. He goes over to* MAMAE *and*

bowing in a fin-de-siècle *style, he asks her to dance. She accepts, now a gracious, coquettish young woman. They dance.*)

MAMAE: Are you Chilean, little domino? Peruvian? From Tacna, little domino? A soldier, perhaps? I know, I've got it. You're a doctor. A lawyer then? Go on, say something to me, give me a clue and I'll guess what you are, you'll see, little domino.

(BELISARIO *says nothing. He merely shakes his head from time to time, giggling nervously as he does so.*)

GRANDMOTHER: (*To* MAMAE, *as if she were still in the armchair*) But wasn't it obvious from the smell? Of course, he probably covered himself with scent, the rascal.

(*The couple dance together with great facility and obvious pleasure. As they dance round the room, the imaginary domino* BELISARIO *is wearing gets caught on some object revealing his bare arm.* MAMAE *shrinks away from him in fright.* BELISARIO *runs to his desk and begins to write, a satisfied look on his face.*)

MAMAE: (*Scared out of her wits*) A negro. A negro. The little domino was a negro. Aaah! Aaah! Aaah!

GRANDMOTHER: Stop screaming like that, Elvira. It reminds me of the awful hullabaloo you made that night at the Choral Society Ball. The orchestra stopped playing, people stopped dancing, the spectators all got up from their seats. There was total pandemonium! You had to be taken home with an attack of nerves. And the party came to a shuddering halt, all because of that blessed negro.

MAMAE: (*Frightened*) Carmen! Carmencita! Look, there, by the bronze fountain in the square. What are they doing to him? Are they beating him?

GRANDMOTHER: It's true. The gentlemen took him out to the street and started laying into him with their canes. Yes, it was by the bronze fountain. What a memory, Elvira!

MAMAE: Stop beating him! He's all covered in blood! He didn't do anything to me. He didn't even speak to me! Aunt Amelia, they'll listen to you! Uncle Menelao, stop them! Stop them beating him! (*Recovering*) Do you think they've killed him, Carmencita?

GRANDMOTHER: No, they just gave him a thrashing for being so impertinent. Then they sent him off to the Chilean gaol. The audacity of it, though. Imagine getting all dressed up like that and slinking into the Choral Society Ball. We were really quite shocked. We used to have nightmares – every night we thought he might come after us through the window. It was the only thing we talked about for weeks – months afterwards. The negro from La Mar.
(BELISARIO *is very excited – he strikes the table. He stops writing and kisses his hand and his pencil.*)

BELISARIO: The negro from La Mar! He's taking shape, he's moving, he's walking!

MAMAE: He's not from La Mar. He's one of the slaves from the Moquegua estate.

GRANDMOTHER: What nonsense, Elvira. There weren't any slaves left in Peru at that time.

MAMAE: Of course there were. My father had three.

BELISARIO: (*Interrupting his work for a moment*) The Mandingos!

MAMAE: They used to ferry me across the Caplina; they'd make a seat with their arms and carry me across from bank to bank.

BELISARIO: (*Writing*) They slept in the byre with their ankles tethered so they couldn't run away.

MAMAE: I didn't see his face, but there was something about the way he moved, something about his eyes, that made me recognize him. I'm convinced he was one of them. A Mandingo on the run . . .
(*The street door opens and* GRANDFATHER *comes in, panting. His hair is ruffled, and his clothing rumpled. He is poorly dressed. The minute she sees him,* MAMAE *acknowledges him with a gracious little bow as if she were greeting some unknown dignitary, and retires into her own imaginary world once again. Enter* AMELIA.)

AMELIA: (*Who has clearly been busy in the kitchen*) Papa . . . What on earth has happened?

GRANDMOTHER: (*Getting up*) Your hat, Pedro? And your walking stick?

GRANDFATHER: They've been stolen.

GRANDMOTHER: Gracious me, how did it happen?

(AMELIA *and* GRANDMOTHER *take* GRANDFATHER *to the armchair and sit him down.*)

GRANDFATHER: As I was getting off the tram. One of those vagrants that loaf around the streets of Lima. Threw me to the ground. He also snatched my . . . (*Searching for the word*) my thingumajig.

GRANDMOTHER: Your watch? Oh, Pedro, they didn't steal your watch as well!

AMELIA: You see we're right, Papa. You're not to go out alone, catching buses and getting on to trams. Why won't you listen? I've told you so many times not to go out in the street, I'm quite hoarse.

GRANDMOTHER: Besides, you're not well. What if you have another blackout? I don't know how you haven't learnt your lesson after such an awful shock. Don't you remember? You were wandering about for hours trying to find the house.

GRANDFATHER: I'm not spending the rest of my life cooped up here, waiting to be carted off feet first, my dear. I'm not going to let this country do away with me just like that . . .

GRANDMOTHER: Did you hurt yourself? Where did you get hit?

GRANDFATHER: Because people who want to work are wasted here in Peru. It's not like that anywhere else in the world. Here, it's a crime to be old. In civilized countries. Like Germany. Or England. It's quite the reverse. Elderly people are consulted, their experience is put to good use. Here they're just tossed on the rubbish tip. Well, I don't hold with it because I know I could do a better job of work than anyone half my age.

(BELISARIO *stops writing.*)

BELISARIO: (*Lost in recollection*) Always rabbiting on about the same old thing; it really got under your skin, didn't it, Grandpa? It was something you never forgot.

(*He tries to carry on with his writing but after scribbling a few lines, his mind starts to wander and he becomes increasingly interested in what is going on in his grandparents' house.*)

AMELIA: You won't solve anything by getting so worked up. You'll only ruin your nerves.

GRANDMOTHER: You've got a weak head, Pedro dear. Do try to understand. The doctor's warned you, if you don't take things more calmly you'll have another attack.

GRANDFATHER: My head's perfectly all right now. I promise you it is. I haven't been feeling the slightest bit dizzy lately. (*With a mournful expression*) I don't care about the hat and the . . . the thingumajig. But I do about the watch. I'd had it for more than fifteen years and it never went wrong once. Anyway, let's change the subject. Did you listen to the eight o'clock serial?

GRANDMOTHER: I heard it, yes. Amelia missed it though because she was doing the ironing for our budding little lawyer here. Imagine, Sister Fatima has left the convent to marry the composer.

AMELIA: Oh look, you've got a cut on your wrist.

GRANDMOTHER: Attacking an old man, really, what a cowardly thing to do.

GRANDFATHER: He came up behind me and caught me off guard. If he'd come at me from the front, it would have been a different story. I may be old, but I've got my pride and I know how to look after myself. (*Smiles.*) I was always good at fighting. At the Jesuit School, in Arequipa, they used to call me 'Sparky', because I'd challenge anyone at the slightest provocation. No one dared trample on my heels.

MAMAE: (*Turning towards them in alarm*) What's that you said, Pedro? You're going to challenge Federico Barreto for writing that poem? Don't! Don't be so hot-headed. He was only being gallant; he didn't mean any harm. Anyway, you'd better not chance it, he's supposed to be an excellent swordsman.

GRANDFATHER: Oh, is he indeed? All right, then I won't. Besides, it was a very inspired piece of poetry. You know you've got to hand it to him, that poet Barreto certainly had good taste. (*To* GRANDMOTHER) He used to flirt with you too, the dirty old man!

GRANDMOTHER: That Elvira, really, the things she comes up with . . . Come, I'm going to put some mercurochrome on you, so you won't get infected.

AMELIA: Let it be a lesson to you, Papa. I'm warning you, I won't ever let you go out alone again – my brothers have strictly forbidden it. At least, not at night. Go for your walks during the day, if you must, but don't go too far, just round the block. Or wait until I can go with you, or Belisario.

GRANDFATHER: (*Getting up*) Very well, Amelia. (*To* GRANDMOTHER) You realize, Carmen, the country must be in a pretty poor state for people to rob an old beggar like me? Fancy risking prison for a rickety old walking stick and a moth-eaten hat that's going yellow round the edges.

GRANDMOTHER: (*Taking him to the inner part of the house*) You were given that watch by the High Court Judges in Piura, when you were Governor there. What a shame, it was such a lovely memento! Oh well, I expect your grandson, Belisario, will give you another one, when he wins his first lawsuit . . .

(*They leave, followed by* AMELIA. *The stage goes dark.*)

BELISARIO: My first lawsuit . . . You too, Grandma, used to have these flights of fancy. (*Flying into a rage*) And what, may I ask, is Grandmother doing here? And are you seriously going to put Grandfather Pedro into a love story when there hasn't even been a kiss yet? You couldn't write it, Belisario. You can't write. You've spent your whole life writing and it gets worse each time. Why is that, Grandpa? A doctor can remove fifty appendixes, cut out two hundred tonsils, trepan a thousand craniums, and then do all these things practically blindfold, isn't that so? Why, then, after writing fifty or a hundred stories is it still just as difficult, just as impossible as it was the first time? Even worse than the first time! A thousand times more difficult than the first time! Grandfather, Grandma: just disappear, will you! Stop distracting me, stop interrupting me, get out of my way. To hell with the pair of you! Let me write my love story! (*Becoming pensive*) Grandfather

26

might have been a character in a novel. One of the lives
of the century: from gradual ruin to irrevocable decline.
Governor of Piura in Bustamente's Constitutional
Government. Former cotton entrepreneur in Santa Cruz
de la Sierra, in Bolivia. Before that, an agricultural
administrator in Camaná. And before that, an employee of
a British firm in Arequipa. But you'd have liked to have
been a lawyer and a poet, wouldn't you, Grandpa? And
you might have been too, if your father hadn't died when
you were fifteen. That's why you were destined for the bar,
Belisario, to carry on the family legal tradition.
(*From the expression on his face, it is clear that a new idea
has started to form in his mind – in connection with what he is
writing. He picks up his pencil, turns it round, adjusts his
papers.*)
Yes, it might work. Come back here, Grandpa, I'm sorry
I told you to go to hell. I love you very much, you know
I do, you're an obvious fictional character. That's why you
always featured in Mamaé's stories. You were the
prototype of all those splendid specimens she was so fond
of, those magnificent, improbable creatures akin to
unicorns and centaurs: gentlemen. (*Writes now with great
enthusiasm.*) But there was nothing mythical about
Grandfather's life. He had to work like a mule, because he
not only had his own children to feed, but also those
people who Grandmother Carmencita – surely the most
charitable woman ever born – kept bringing in from all
over the place. Whether they were the children of
nincompoops who'd blown out their brains playing
Russian roulette to win some bet or other, or eligible young
ladies with no father or mother, such as Mamaé.
(*As the lights come up, we find* SEÑORA CARLOTA *on stage.*
MAMAE, *from her armchair, looks her over respectfully. She
gets up – a young woman once again – and goes towards her.*)
MAMAE: Good afternoon, Señora Carlota, what a surprise. My
aunt and uncle are out at the moment; so is Carmencita.
Do sit down, please. May I offer you a cup of tea?
SEÑORA CARLOTA: 'Just as if she'd stepped out of a watercolour

by Maestro Modesto Molina.' I heard somebody saying
that about you at the Alameda, at the open air concert. It's
true, you're just like that.

MAMAE: You're very kind, Señora Carlota.

SEÑORA CARLOTA: Raven hair, porcelain skin. Manicured
hands, and such dainty feet. Yes, the perfect little doll.

MAMAE: For goodness' sake, señora, you're making me blush.
Won't you sit down? Uncle and Aunt won't be long. They
went to express their condolences to . . .

SEÑORA CARLOTA: Young, pretty and, besides, a considerable
inheritance in the offing, am I right? It is true, isn't it,
that the plantation your father had in Moquegua is being
held in trust for you until you come of age?

MAMAE: Why are you saying all these things to me? And why
that tone of voice? You're talking as if you were angry
with me for some reason.

SEÑORA CARLOTA: Anger isn't quite the word, my sensitive
little flower. I'm not angry with you. I hate you. I hate
you with all my power and all my mind. All year I've been
willing on you the worst possible disasters. That you'd
get run over by a train. That your face would be eaten
away by smallpox. That your lungs would be racked with
tuberculosis. That the devil would take you!

MAMAE: But what have I ever done to you, Señora Carlota? I
hardly even know you. Why are you saying such dreadful
things to me? And here was I thinking you were coming
to give me a wedding present.

SEÑORA CARLOTA: I've come to tell you that Joaquín doesn't
love you. He loves me. You may be younger. You may
be a virgin, you may still be unmarried! But he doesn't
like delicate little ornaments that blow over in the wind.
He likes me. Because I know something young ladies like
you will never learn. I know how to love. I know what
passion is. I know how to give pleasure and how to receive
it. Yes, it's a naughty word for you, isn't it? Pleasure.

MAMAE: You've taken leave of your senses, Señora Carlota.
You're forgetting . . .

SEÑORA CARLOTA: That I'm married and I've got three

28

children? I haven't forgotten. I don't give a damn! Not
for my husband, my children, Tacna society, the Church
– they can say what they like – I don't give a damn!
That's love, you see. I'm prepared to do anything, rather
than lose the man I love.

MAMAE: If it is as you say, if Joaquín does love you, why has
he asked me to marry him?

SEÑORA CARLOTA: For your name, for the plantation you're
going to inherit, because an officer has to safeguard his
future. But, above all, because he can't marry the woman
he loves. He's marrying you because it's convenient. He's
resigned himself to marrying you. Did you hear that? He's
re-signed to it. He's told me so himself, hundreds of
times. Only today in fact – not two hours ago. Yes, I've
just come from being with Joaquín. I can still hear the
sound of his voice echoing in my ears: 'You're the only
one who can really give me pleasure, my soldier's girl.'
That's what he calls me, you see, when I abandon myself
to him: his soldier's girl, his little soldier's girl.

MAMAE: Señora Carlota, you've gone quite far enough. Please,
I beg you . . .

SEÑORA CARLOTA: I'm shocking you, I know. But I don't care.
I've come to make it quite clear to you that I'm not going
to give Joaquín up, even if he does marry you. And he
won't give me up either. We're going to carry on seeing
each other behind your back. I've come to tell you what
your life will be like, after you're married. Every morning,
every afternoon, wondering if your husband's really gone
to the barracks – or if he's making love with me instead.

MAMAE: I'm calling the servants to show you to the door, Señora
Carlota.

SEÑORA CARLOTA: And if Joaquín is transferred, I'll leave my
husband and my children and I'll follow him. So all your
doubts and torments will continue. I've come just so that
you know how far a woman in love is prepared to go. Do
you see?

MAMAE: Yes, señora. I see. Maybe it is true what you say. I'd
never be capable of behaving like that myself. For me,

love could never be a disease. I can't understand you.
You're beautiful, elegant, and your husband such a
distinguished man – the whole of Tacna respects him. And
such lovely little children too. What more can anyone
want in life?

SEÑORA CARLOTA: All right, maybe that's how you see it. But
all these things you seem to hanker after, I'd gladly
sacrifice the lot, just for one word from Joaquín. I'd risk
hell if that's the price I have to pay to go on seeing him.

MAMAE: I'm sure God will be listening to you, Señora Carlota.

SEÑORA CARLOTA: Then he'll know I'm telling the truth. When
Joaquín holds me in his arms, when he hugs me and
subjects me to his little whims, nothing else in the world
seems to exist any more: not my husband, my children,
my reputation, or even God. Only him. And you're not
going to take that away from me.

MAMAE: How long have you been Joaquín's . . . Joaquín's lady-
friend?

SEÑORA CARLOTA: His mistress? Two years. And I'm going to
tell you something else. We see each other every week in
a little hut in La Mar. At sunset. When the negroes return
singing from the plantations. We always hear them. We
know all their songs by heart we've heard them so often.
What else would you like to know?

MAMAE: Nothing, señora. I'd be grateful if you'd leave now.

SEÑORA CARLOTA: You could never live with Joaquín. You're
too pure for such a hot-blooded man. He says so himself.
Go and find yourself some tepid youth somewhere. You
could never be a soldier's girl – not to Joaquín or to
anyone. You're too insipid, you're not flirtatious enough,
you haven't got the imagination.

MAMAE: You must go this instant! My aunt and uncle will be
back at any moment, señora!

SEÑORA CARLOTA: Let them see me, for all I care. Let the
scandal break out once and for all.

MAMAE: It won't be my fault if it does. I've heard nothing; I
know nothing, and I don't want to know anything either.

SEÑORA CARLOTA: And yet, you've heard everything; you know

everything. And now it'll start to nag away at you like a little worm gnawing at your heart. 'Is he really only marrying me because it suits him?' 'Is he really in love with her?' 'Does he really call her his soldier's girl when he holds her in his arms?'

(SEÑORA CARLOTA *leaves.* BELISARIO, *who at the beginning of the dialogue between* SEÑORA CARLOTA *and* MAMAE *was writing, making notes and throwing papers on the floor, has suddenly become pensive, and has been taking more and more interest in what the two women are saying. He finally goes over to* MAMAE's *armchair, where he sits crouching like a child.* MAMAE *talks to herself as she goes back towards her armchair. She has become an old woman again.*)

MAMAE: Did he really tell her I was a sensitive little flower? A little prude who'll never be able to make him happy like she can? Was he really with her yesterday? Is he with her now? Will he be with her again tomorrow?
(*She sits huddled in her chair.* BELISARIO *is at her feet, listening to her like a little child.*)

BELISARIO: So the wicked woman made the young bride terribly jealous.

MAMAE: It was worse than that. She caused her great distress and alarm, and filled her innocent little head with all sorts of monstrous thoughts so that her brain seethed with vipers and vultures.

BELISARIO: What sort of vultures, Mamaé? Turkey buzzards?

MAMAE: (*Continuing the story*) And the poor young lady, her eyes filled with tears, couldn't help thinking, 'So he doesn't love me for myself but for my name and my family's position in Tacna. That young man I'm so much in love with is nothing but an unscrupulous scoundrel.'

BELISARIO: But I don't believe that, Mamaé. Whoever heard of anyone getting married just for a name or a social position! He might have wanted to marry the young lady because she was going to inherit a plantation – now that I can believe, but as for the rest of it . . .

MAMAE: The story about the plantation wasn't true. The

Chilean officer knew that it had been auctioned off in
order to pay the debts of the young lady's father.

BELISARIO: Now you're muddling the story up, Mamaé.

MAMAE: You see the Chilean officer had lied to the wicked
woman. About the young lady inheriting a plantation. So
that the story about marrying for money rather than love
would seem more convincing. In fact he wasn't just
deceiving the young lady, he was deceiving Señora Carlota
as well.

BELISARIO: Was the wicked woman called Carlota?

MAMAE: Yes. But she had a most unattractive nickname. They
used to call her 'The Soldier's Woman.'

BELISARIO: What is a soldier's woman, Mamaé?

MAMAE: Ach, it's a nasty expression. (*Her mind wandering,
talking as if to herself*) But she wasn't stupid, she came
out with a few home truths. Such as: 'A woman can only
keep her pride if she renounces love.'

BELISARIO: You're off on your own again, Mamaé. You've left
me dangling in mid-air.

(*He gets to his feet and goes back to his desk, muttering to
himself, while* MAMAE's *lips keep on moving for a moment,
as if she were carrying on with the story. Then she falls asleep.*)
The wicked woman . . . No story was ever complete
without one. And a very good thing too. There should
always be wicked women in romantic stories. Don't be
afraid, Belisario, take a tip from your old Mamaé. Besides,
paper doesn't discriminate, you can write anything you
like on it. So fill the story with wicked women, they're
always so much more interesting. There were two of
them, weren't there, Mamaé? Sometimes she was called
Carlota and she was a mischievous woman who lived in
Tacna at the beginning of the century. And sometimes she
was an Indian woman from Camaná, who had been
thrashed by a gentleman for some mysterious reason during
the twenties. (*Starts to write.*) They often got mixed up or
overlapped, and then there was that mother-of-pearl fan
which suddenly started to feature in the stories – the one
some romantic poet had scribbled a few hasty lines on.

GRANDMOTHER: (*Coming in*) Elvira! Elvira! But what have you done? Have you gone quite mad? Your wedding dress! I don't believe it! All that beautiful lace embroidery, and that veil – so fine and delicate it was almost like foam!

MAMAE: It took half a box of matches and I burnt the ends of my fingers. Eventually I thought of putting a little paraffin on it. It went up all right then.

GRANDMOTHER: (*Distressed*) But the wedding is tomorrow. We've got people coming all the way from Moquegua, Iquique, and Arica. You haven't had a row with Joaquín? Really, Elvirita, on the day before your wedding. You mean the house has been festooned with lilies and roses all for nothing? And we've spent a month preparing sweets and pastries just for the fun of it? They've just brought the wedding cake.

MAMAE: Has it got three tiers? Like the one in that novel by Gustave Flaubert? With marzipan columns and almond Cupids? Oh, we simply must eat it even if I don't get married. That Italian, Máspoli, is bound to have gone to so much trouble, he's always so sweet to me.

GRANDMOTHER: Well, aren't you going to tell me what happened? We've never had any secrets from each other. Why did you burn your wedding dress?

MAMAE: Because I don't want to get married any more.

GRANDMOTHER: But why? You and Joaquín seemed so happy together – up until last night anyway. What's he done to you?

MAMAE: Nothing. I've discovered I'm just not interested in marriage. I prefer to remain single.

GRANDMOTHER: How do you mean, you're just not interested in marriage? You can't fool me, Elvirita. Every girl wants to marry, it's her one ambition in life and you're no exception. We grew up dreaming about the day we'd have our own homes, guessing what our husbands would look like, choosing names for our children. Have you forgotten that already?

MAMAE: Yes, my dear. I've forgotten all about it.

GRANDMOTHER: You haven't. I don't believe you.

(GRANDMOTHER *and* MAMAE *carry on their conversation silently.* BELISARIO *has stopped writing for a moment. He looks pensive, absorbed in his own thoughts. When he speaks, it is as if he were watching them and listening to what they say.*)

BELISARIO: Their houses were both going to be as spotless and tidy as the British Consul's. They were both going to have maids who would always be impeccably dressed in well-starched pinafores and bonnets; Grandma and Mamaé were going to send them off to catechism and make them say their rosaries along with the family. They would make sure that they always looked beautiful so that their husbands would remain in love with them and not be unfaithful to them. They would bring up their sons like gallant young men and their daughters like eligible young women. Grandmother was going to have four, Mamaé six, eight . . .

(*He starts to write again.*)

MAMAE: He doesn't even know I'm not going to marry him. He was going to Isaiah's, the tailor, today, to collect his dress uniform for the wedding. He's going to get quite a surprise when the servants tell him he can't ever set foot inside this house again.

GRANDMOTHER: (*Embarrassed*) Is it because you're frightened, Elvirita? I mean, frightened of . . . of your wedding night?

(MAMAE *shakes her head.*)

Then why? Something dreadful must have happened for you to break off your engagement the day before your wedding . . .

MAMAE: I've already told you. I've changed my mind. I'm not going to get married. Not to Joaquín or anyone else.

GRANDMOTHER: Is it God then? Is that it? Are you going into the convent?

MAMAE: No, I've no vocation to be a nun. I'm not getting married and I'm not going into the convent either. I'm going to carry on as I have done up to now. Single and unattached.

GRANDMOTHER: You're hiding something important from me, Elvira. Remain single indeed! But it's the most dreadful thing that can happen to a girl. Look at Aunt Hilaria. You say yourself that she makes your hair stand on end, she's so lonely. No husband, no home of her own, no children, and half mad. Do you really want to end up like her, and have to face old age like a soul in torment?

MAMAE: Better to live alone than with the wrong person, Carmencita. The only thing I'm sorry about is the anxiety I'm going to cause Aunt Amelia and Uncle Menelao. (GRANDMOTHER *nods*.) Did they see the dress burning? They're so sensitive and sweet. They haven't even come to ask me why I set fire to it. And they went to such trouble so I could have a wedding to end all weddings. They've certainly earned their place in heaven, they're so kind . . .

GRANDMOTHER: (*Giving her a kiss on the cheek*) You'll never be left alone like Aunt Hilaria. Because when I get married, that is if any gentleman cares to have me, you'll come and live with us.

MAMAE: You're so good to me, my dear.
(*They are both overcome with emotion and kiss each other. BELISARIO gets to his feet and walks across the stage with a pile of papers in his hand. He seems restless.*)

BELISARIO: Well, it won't be a love story, but it's certainly romantic. That much is clear. As far back as you can remember, and as far back as my mother could remember, you were both as thick as thieves. But all those years of living in the same house, wasn't there ever any friction, any jealousy between them? They shared their lives, but didn't they ever feel envious of each other? (*He looks sardonically at them both.*) Well, I don't suppose you actually shared Grandfather. But you certainly shared the children, didn't you?
(*He walks round GRANDMOTHER and MAMAE, looking at them carefully.*
That is to say, you produced them, Grandma, but it was you, Mamaé, who had all the anxiety and the sleepless

35

nights. You gave them their bottles and changed their
nappies and watched over their cradles, and it was you
who stayed at home so that Grandmother and Grandfather
could go to the theatre or the cinema, or to parties, when
they were still able to afford such luxuries.

(*He goes towards the desk, where he leaves his papers and
pencils. He rolls up his trousers, like a child about to wade
across a stream, and suddenly starts to skip and jump about,
as if he were spinning a top or playing hopscotch.*)

But there was someone else you were even more patient
with, Mamaé – infinitely patient with in fact – and that
was that budding little lawyer, over in Bolivia – yes, the
future saviour of the family.

(*During* BELISARIO's *speech,* AGUSTIN *and* CESAR *have come
in from the street. They kiss* GRANDMOTHER *and their sister,*
AMELIA, *and go up to greet* MAMAE, *who smiles politely and
bows when she sees them coming. They embrace her. She lets
them, but suddenly shouts out:*)

MAMAE: Long live Herod! Long live Herod! Ahhh!

(*As* MAMAE *shouts,* BELISARIO *carries on writing. He seems
to be enjoying himself very much. In fact he is so delighted
he can hardly sit still. He stops working from time to time to
observe* MAMAE. *He imitates her gestures and expressions –
he raises his hand to his throat as if he were attempting to
throttle someone.*)

GRANDMOTHER: Quiet, Elvira, stop shouting like a maniac.
What's this stupid habit you've got of shrieking 'Long live
Herod!' whenever Agustín and César appear? (*To* AGUSTIN
and CESAR) Dear oh dear, what with Mamaé who lives in
a world of her own, and my husband who doesn't
remember anything from one moment to the next, I don't
know what's to become of me, I really don't. I'm just going
to see if Pedro's awake. He went to have a little rest.

(*She goes out.* AMELIA, AGUSTIN *and* CESAR *gather round*
MAMAE.)

MAMAE: Of all the characters in history, he's quite my favourite.
He had every one of the little blighters killed. I'd do the

same – I'd do away with the lot of them. I wouldn't leave
a single one, not even as a specimen.

CESAR: (*To his brother*) And there were you wanting me to get
the children out of the car so they could say hello to
Mama and Papa.

MAMAE: Because I loathe them! And do you know why? Because
of all those thousands and thousands of dirty nappies.

AGUSTIN: (*Stroking her hair*) You've spent your life looking after
other people's children, and now it turns out you detest
the little mites.

MAMAE: Because of those millions of bibs they're sick over,
they're always about to burst into tears – they're always
drooling, their noses need wiping, and their knees are
always dirty and covered in scabs. And they won't even
let the grown-ups have their meals in peace, what with
their bad table manners and naughty little pranks.
(MAMAE *talks to them calmly, smiling and bowing, but she
gives the impression that she neither hears nor understands a
word of what they say.*)

AMELIA: And to think that when Belisario had chickenpox, she
was the one who threw me out of the room so that she
could sleep beside him.

MAMAE: Because they shout and throw tantrums; everything
gets broken, mucked up, or ruined.

BELISARIO: (*Interrupting his work*) You'd spend the day covering
me with that ghastly black ointment. Every little spot,
one by one. Then you'd take me by the hands and tell me
stories to take my mind off it so I wouldn't scratch. But
even that didn't stop me looking a sight, Mamaé!

MAMAE: They're selfish little brutes, they don't care about
anyone. They're like sultans, you've got to pander to all
their stupid little fads. So, like Herod, every single one of
them. Like so, and like so!

CESAR: What about that time in Arequipa, Mamaé, when I'd
invite my schoolmates home? You used to make tea for
all thirty of us, remember? So you can swear you hate
children till you're blue in the face, I just don't believe
it.

(AMELIA *signals to* AGUSTIN *and they both move aside a few steps.* BELISARIO *is sitting at his desk. He looks on intrigued, as* AMELIA *and* AGUSTIN *talk.*)

AMELIA: I want to have a word with you, Agustín.

AGUSTIN: Yes, Amelia.

AMELIA: I've been meaning to tell you, I . . . I can't go on like this any more.

(*When* CESAR *hears her, he goes up to them.* MAMAE *falls asleep.*)

CESAR: What's the matter, Amelia?

AMELIA: I'm quite exhausted. You'll just have to take on a maid.

AGUSTIN: We'd have done that some time ago if it had been at all possible. I thought we agreed that César and I would help Belisario finish his course at university and you would look after the house.

AMELIA: Yes, I know. But I can't go on like this, Agustín. It's too much work for one person. And besides I'm slowly going out of my mind in this crazy household. What with Father and Mother and Mamaé – they're all getting so old now. And Father doesn't remember a single thing. I give him his lunch, he eats it, and five minutes later he asks for it all over again. And if I don't do exactly as he wants, Mother bursts into tears.

CESAR: Don't talk so loud, Amelia. Mamaé will hear you.

AMELIA: Let her hear me; she doesn't understand. Her mind's completely gone, César. (*Looks at* MAMAE.) Not to mention her body. God knows I'm patient, and I'm very fond of her. But there are limits. Can't you see she's like a child? Washing her knickers and her dirty nighties has become a nightmare. Then there's the cooking, the cleaning, the ironing, the beds to be made and the dishes to be washed. I just can't cope any more.

CESAR: (*To* AGUSTIN) Perhaps we really should consider taking on a maid, after all.

AGUSTIN: Oh, that's brilliant, César. Yes, why don't we? You'd be paying for her, I suppose.

CESAR: There's no need to be sarcastic, Agustín. You know I'm hard up at the moment.

AGUSTIN: Then don't talk about taking on a maid. Have you any idea what it costs to run this house? Has it ever occurred to you to pick up a pencil and work it out? Well, there's the rent, the housekeeping, the water rates, the electricity, dustmen, doctor's bills, medicine, not to mention the three thousand for Amelia. Do you know how much it all comes to? Fourteen or fifteen thousand *soles* a month. And what do you contribute apart from belly-aching the whole time? Two thousand *soles*. (JOAQUIN *comes in, as discreetly as a ghost, dressed in the same uniform he was wearing at the beginning of the play. He sits down next to* MAMAE.)

CESAR: It's hard enough for me to manage the two thousand. I don't even earn enough to cover my own expenses. I'm in constant debt, as you well know . . . I've got four children, Agustín. I've had to put the two younger ones into a state school this year, along with all the mestizos and the negroes . . .

MAMAE: (*Opening her eyes*) The mestizos . . . Yes, it was there, every evening, just when the labourers were returning from the plantations. In the suburb, where the mestizos and the negroes live. In the shanties of La Mar.

AMELIA: You don't imagine I spend those three thousand *soles* you give me on myself, do you, Agustín? Every cent goes on Belisario's education. I can't even buy myself a handkerchief. I've even given up smoking, to save you any more expense.

BELISARIO: (*Looking at the audience, exaggerating*) Me, get a job? No, mother, it's out of the question. What about the statutory regulations? What about the civil code? The constitutions? The laws of contract? Written law? Common law? I thought you wanted me to become famous so I'd be able to help you all out one day? Well, you've got to give me more money for books then! How cynical you could be at times, Belisario.

AGUSTIN: But Belisario could always get a part-time job,

Amelia. Hundreds of university students do. You know I've always supported your son – and you, ever since your husband killed himself in that stupid way. But things have become very tough recently, and Belisario is quite grown up now. Let me look for a job for him.

CESAR: No, Agustín, Amelia's right. He must be allowed to finish at the university first. Or he'll go the same way as I did. I gave up studying to start a job and look at the result. But he was always top of the class. He's bound to go far. He needs a degree though, because nowadays . . . (*His voice fades down to a whisper, as* MAMAE's *voice comes to the fore.*)

MAMAE: I've often been past those shanties. With Uncle Menelao and Aunt Amelia, on the way to the sea. Negroes, mestizos and Indians would come up to us, begging. They'd put their hands right inside the carriage and I remember Uncle Menelao saying: 'What revolting nails they have.' I used to be so frightened of them. La Mar looks pretty from a distance with its thatched huts and sandy streets. But when you're there, you can see that it's poor, dirty and smelly and it's full of savage dogs. So it was there you used to meet her.

JOAQUIN: Yes. There. In La Mar. Every evening. We'd meet and watch the sun going down. (*The conversation between* AGUSTIN, AMELIA *and* CESAR *now comes to the fore.*)

AGUSTIN: Everyone has his reasons, of course. Well, I've got mine too. You see, I could say I was fed up with living in lodgings, travelling by bus, and not being able to get married. Ever since the day I started work, over half my salary has been going towards helping Mother and Father, not to mention Amelia and my nephew. I could say I was fed up never being able to go to a good restaurant, never having any holidays, and always having to have my suits repaired. And because I'm fed up, from now on I'm only going to contribute two thousand *soles* a month towards the upkeep of this house. The same as you. What then would happen to Father and Mother and Mamaé – and what would happen to our future legal genius?

AMELIA: Don't be so scornful, Agustín. My son will be a great lawyer one day, you'll see, he'll have masses of clients and he'll earn a fortune. I'm not sending him out to work until he finishes his studies. He won't be a failure and a mediocrity.

AGUSTIN: Like me, you mean.

MAMAE: So every evening, after your guard duty, as I waited for you, saying rosary after rosary to make the time pass more quickly, you were already on your way to her, to La Mar, where you'd talk passionately to her for hours.

JOAQUIN: My little soldier's girl, my love, your hands – they're so strong – and yet so soft and gentle. Hold my head here, at the temples, I've been riding all morning and my body is throbbing. Press a little harder. It's so soothing. That's right. Ah yes, I feel as if my head were sinking into a bed of jasmine.

BELISARIO: You saw straight through me, didn't you, Uncle Agustín?

CESAR: No. Please, don't start up again. It's the same thing day after day. Hasn't it caused enough bad blood as it is? Instead of arguing, why don't you think seriously about what I suggested?

AMELIA: I have, César. I'm ready to go along with it. I was against it at first, but I've changed my mind.

CESAR: Of course, Amelia. It's the only sensible thing to do. (Looks at MAMAE.) She's already living in another world; she won't even notice the change. You'll be more relaxed; you'll have more time for Mother and Father. They'll live more comfortably. And it's even quite likely that Mamaé will be happier, too.

(JOAQUIN has taken hold of MAMAE's hands; he kisses them passionately.)

JOAQUIN: But there's something else about you, Carlota, something I like even more than your hands.

MAMAE: (Frightened) What? What else was it you liked about that woman?

AGUSTIN: So we put Mamaé into a home, do we? I see. Do you really think that's going to solve things. Of course it's very easy. Especially when you're all no doubt thinking of that private place, San Isidro, where Aunt Augusta was. I'm sure Mamaé would be fine there. It's so clean, and they've got nurses looking after the old people day and night, they take them out for walks in the gardens. They even show them a film once a week, don't they? (*Sarcastically*) Have you any idea how much that place costs?

JOAQUIN: Your neck. Let me kiss it, let me smell your sweetness. Yes. Yes, that's right. Now I want to kiss your ears, put my tongue into those snug little lairs, nibble those pink little lobes. That's why I love you, my little soldier's girl. You know how to give me pleasure. You're not like Elvira, that passionless dummy. She thinks love is all about reading poetry by an idiot who calls himself Federico Barreto.

AGUSTIN: Mamaé wouldn't go to San Isidro. She'd go to the Beneficencia, which is free. You don't know about that place, do you? But I've taken the trouble to go and see it. The old people there all live on top of each other in the most filthy conditions. They hardly even have any clothes to wear. They're eaten alive by lice, and they sleep on the floor on sacks. What's more, it's in Santo Cristo next to the cemetery so that the old people spend all day watching funerals. Do you really want to send Mamaé there?

MAMAE: (*Very distressed, almost in tears*) We weren't yet married, Joaquín. I couldn't let you lose respect for me. It would have lowered me in your eyes. It was for you I did it, for you. So that you would have a wife you wouldn't be ashamed of.

CESAR: And do you really think Mamaé lives well here? Have you lost all sense of smell, Agustín. You say yourself that every time you have to have a cup of milk in this house, it practically turns your stomach. You must understand I'm not suggesting the home out of spite or anything, but to save you expense. I love her as much as you do.

MAMAE: And what was so wrong about the poetry? That's how things were in those days. When a woman was in love she read poetry. That's what young ladies and gentlemen did, Joaquín. Federico Barreto was certainly no fool. He was a great poet. All the girls in Tacna were dying of envy when he wrote those lines on my fan.

AMELIA: (*To* AGUSTIN) Do you think I've no feelings? I'm the one who baths her, puts her to bed, dresses her; I'm the one who feeds her, don't forget. But . . . you're right. We can't send Mamaé there. Besides, it's true – Mother would never agree to it.

JOAQUIN: What a wonderful couple we'd have made, my little soldier's girl. Such a pity you're married! When I think of that frigid little saint . . . I ask myself, will she be capable of satisfying me, when I feel those waves of passion welling up inside me as I do now, ready to break at any moment? (*Speaking in her ear*) Shall I tell you what I'm going to do to Elvira when she's my wife?

MAMAE: (*Covering her ears*) No! No! I don't want to know.

CESAR: All right. Then I'm sorry I even spoke. Let's forget about the home. I'm only trying to help, to throw out a few ideas. And all you do is to make me feel worthless.

JOAQUIN: With these hands . . . I'll undress her. I'll take off her bridal veil, her dress, her petticoat, her bodice. Her shoes. Her stockings. Slowly, watching her blush, not knowing what to say, what to do, where to look. A young girl overcome with shyness and fear is an exciting prospect.

AGUSTIN: Come down to earth, César. You're not going to solve the problem with brainless suggestions. If, instead of all these far-fetched schemes, you were to give me another five hundred *soles* towards the running of this house, you really would be helping.

(*Throughout the scene,* BELISARIO *has been writing at his desk. He has also been listening and observing his family,* MAMAE *and* JOAQUIN. *He now starts to yawn. He works more and more reluctantly.*)

JOAQUIN: And when her skin starts to quiver with fear, as I gradually uncover it, I'll lean over, and smell it, taste it, cover it with feverish kisses. Are you jealous my little soldier's girl? Can you see me running my hands, my eyes, my lips over that tender little body? Can you see her trembling, her eyes closed. Are you jealous? I want you to be jealous, Carlota.

MAMAE: I'm not listening to you. I'm covering my ears, I'm shutting you out. I'm closing my eyes, I don't want to see you either. You can't insult me however hard you try, you're not going to drag me down to your common level. Oh, this crazy little head . . .

(*She hits her head as if punishing it for giving her these hallucinations.*)

AMELIA: Quiet now, Father's coming.

(*Enter* GRANDFATHER *and* GRANDMOTHER. AGUSTIN *and* CESAR *come forward to kiss their father.* BELISARIO *has put down his pen. He rests for a moment, his head on his arm.*)

BELISARIO: (*Yawning*) The world won't come to an end because you can't finish a story, Belisario. Go on, have a little nap.

GRANDFATHER: You got all worked up about nothing. I'm perfectly all right. That . . . that brigand didn't do me any harm. But at least it's got them to pay us a visit. They haven't been here for weeks.

CESAR: But we were here all yesterday afternoon, Father.

JOAQUIN: And then, when she's surrendered herself totally to me, and her body's all wet with my kisses, I'll make her take all my clothes off too. Just as you do. I'll teach her obedience. I'll train her like my horse: so that she'll only allow me to handle her. And while she's undressing me, I'll be thinking about you. About all those things only you know how to do to me. I'll feel my blood getting hotter. I'll put off making love to her till the very last moment, then when I do, I'll be thinking all the time I'm with you, Carlota.

(*He caresses* MAMAE's *breasts.*)

MAMAE: No. No. Go away, get out of here. I won't let you, not even in my wildest dreams, not even when I'm your wife. Aunt Amelia! Uncle Menelao! Carmencita! Ahhh! Ahhh!

(JOAQUIN *disappears, smiling.* AMELIA, AGUSTIN, CESAR, *and the* GRANDPARENTS *turn to look at* MAMAE *when they hear her shouting.*)

GRANDMOTHER: What's the matter, Mamaé? Why do you shout the whole time like a maniac?

MAMAE: (*Suffocating, embarrassed*) I dreamt my fiancé was trying to touch my breasts, Carmencita. These Chileans are so forward! They even take liberties with you in your sleep! These Chileans, really!

(*She crosses herself, horrified.* BELISARIO *has fallen asleep over his papers. His pencil slips out of his hand and falls on to the floor. He starts to snore.*)

ACT TWO

As the curtain rises, the GRANDPARENTS *are listening to the Sunday Mass on the old wireless set they keep in the small drawing room of their house. The voice of the priest drones on monotonously and* GRANDMOTHER *and* MAMAE *genuflect and cross themselves at the appropriate moments.* GRANDFATHER *listens reluctantly. At intervals we hear the tram passing.* AMELIA *is laying the table for supper. She moves in and out of the room without paying any attention to the Mass on the wireless.* BELISARIO, *who has fallen asleep at his desk, slowly wakes up. He yawns, rubs his eyes and reads over something he has written. Suddenly something occurs to him which makes him jump up in great excitement and take hold of the little chair in which he has been sitting. He leans against it like a little old man who can't walk and starts to make his way slowly across the stage, dragging himself along with little hops and skips (exactly as we will see* MAMAE *doing later).*

BELISARIO: That time Grandfather was robbed, could she still
    walk then? Could you, Mamaé? Yes, this was how it was,
    with your little wooden chair, like a child playing gee-gees.
    From your bedroom to the bathroom, from the bathroom
    to the armchair, from the armchair to the dining room,
    and from the dining room back to your bedroom again:
    the geography of your world. (*Reflects; repeats the expression,
    savouring it.*) The geo-gra-phy of your world, Mamaé. I
    like it, Belisario!
    (*He runs to his desk and writes something down. Then he
    starts to chew his pencil, lost in the world of his memories.*)
    Of course you were still walking. You only stopped when
    Grandfather died. 'She hasn't yet realized,' Mama would
    say. 'She doesn't understand,' Uncle César and Uncle
    Agustín would say. (*Looks at* MAMAE.) Did you really not
    realize that in that house that was already so full of ghosts,
    there was now one more to add to its number? Of course
    you did, Mamaé! (*Jots down a few notes on the paper in
    front of him.*) You loved Grandfather very much, didn't
    you, Mamaé? Just how much did you love him? And in

what way? What about that letter? And that thrashing?
And the wicked Indian woman from Camaná? The
gentleman always seemed to be linked to that letter and
that Indian woman in the stories about the young lady
from Tacna. What was behind so mysterious, scandalous,
and sinful a story, Mamaé? Mysterious, scandalous,
sinful! I like it! I like it!
(*He starts to write furiously.*)

AMELIA: (*Who has already served up the soup*) Supper is ready!
(*The Mass has finished and a commercial break has begun
with an advertisement for Chocolate Sublime.* AMELIA *turns
the wireless off. The* GRANDPARENTS *go and sit down at the
table.* GRANDFATHER *seems very downcast.* MAMAE *raises
herself laboriously out of her armchair and takes a little step
forward.* AMELIA *runs to help her.*)
Do you want to break your leg? Where are you going
without your chair, Mamaé?
(*She takes* MAMAE *by the arm and guides her towards the
table.*)

MAMAE: To church. That's where I'm going. To pray. I want
to go to Mass, to confession. I'm sick of listening to Mass
on the wireless. It's not the same. The priest can say what
he likes. It just isn't. Your mind wanders, you can't take
it seriously.
(MAMAE *and* AMELIA *sit down. They start to eat.*)

GRANDMOTHER: Then my husband will have to carry you,
Mamaé. It would take you hours to get to the Church of the
Fatima with that little chair of yours. (*To* GRANDFATHER)
Remember, Pedro, how you used to carry us across the
river when we came to visit you in Camaná? How we used
to scream and yell!
(GRANDFATHER *nods listlessly.*)

AMELIA: What's the matter, Papa? You haven't opened your
mouth all day.

GRANDMOTHER: I try to talk to you and all you do is nod like
one of those giant-headed creatures at Carnival. You make
me feel like an idiot. Are you ill?

GRANDFATHER: No, my little funny face, there's nothing the

matter with me. I'm all right. I was just finishing up
this . . . thingumajig, before it gets cold.

AMELIA: Soup, Papa.

GRANDMOTHER: What's this mania you've got for calling
everything a thingumajig? If you forget what it is, ask. Can't
you see it's soup?

MAMAE: A pig's breakfast, that's what it is.

GRANDFATHER: (*In an effort to speak*) No, it's good. It just
needs a little salt perhaps.

BELISARIO: (*Looking up from his papers*) He thought everything
was good; he called everything a thingumajig, and
everything needed salt. A man who never complained about
anything, except not being able to find work in his old
age. Grandmother, in all the fifty years she'd been married
to him, never heard him raise his voice once. That's why
the thrashing that Indian woman from Camaná got seemed
so inconceivable, Mamaé. In his last few years, salt
became an obsession with him. He put salt in his coffee,
salt on his pudding. And he thought everything was –

GRANDFATHER: Splendid! Splendid!

(BELISARIO *starts to write again*.)

GRANDMOTHER: I know what's wrong with you, Pedro. Before,
when you went out for your little walks, you'd go just to
make sure the outside world was still there. And when
your children stopped you, they took away the one
pleasure you had left in life.

AMELIA: You say it, Mama, as if we'd done it deliberately to
torment him.

GRANDFATHER: Am I complaining?

GRANDMOTHER: It would be a great deal easier if you did.

GRANDFATHER: Right then, if it'll make you any happier, I'll
spend the whole day grumbling. I can't think what about
though, my little funny face.

GRANDMOTHER: I'm not getting at you, dear. Do you think I
enjoy keeping you cloistered up in here? Look, after lunch
we'll go for a walk round the block. I just hope to God my
varicose veins don't start playing me up again.

(AMELIA *gets up and collects the plates.*)

AMELIA: You haven't had your soup, Mamaé.

MAMAE: Soup? A dog's dinner more like – and a rabid one at that!

AMELIA: (*Going out*) If you knew what my brothers gave me for the housekeeping, you'd realize I perform miracles just to get you all two square meals a day.

GRANDMOTHER: Those visits to church . . . Yes, Mamaé, what a consolation they were. We'd go to the Fatima one day, the next to the Carmelites. Do you remember that time we went walking as far as the Parish of Miraflores. We had to stop at every corner, we were so exhausted.

MAMAE: Those negroes singing and dancing in the middle of Mass takes some getting used to. It's like a party. They're such heathens!

(AMELIA *comes in with the second course. She serves the* GRANDPARENTS *and* MAMAE *and sits down.*)

AMELIA: Negroes? In the Parish of Miraflores?

MAMAE: In the Parish of La Mar.

AMELIA: Miraflores, Mamaé.

GRANDMOTHER: She's talking about Tacna, dear. Before you were born. La Mar. A shanty town full of negroes and Indians, on the outskirts of the town. I did some watercolours of La Mar, when I was studying under Maestro Modesto Molina . . .

AMELIA: Mamaé used to go to Mass in a shanty town full of negroes and Indians?

GRANDMOTHER: We went there several times – on Sundays. There was a little timber chapel with reed matting. After Mamaé broke off her engagement, she got it into her head she'd either go to Mass in La Mar or she wouldn't go at all. She could be as stubborn as a mule.

MAMAE: (*Following her own train of thought*) Padre Venancio says it's not a sin, that it's all right for them to dance and sing at Mass. He says God forgives them because they don't know what they're doing. He's one of these avant-garde little priests . . .

GRANDMOTHER: It was wonderful entertainment though, wasn't it, Mamaé? All those Masses and Novenas, all those

Holy Week processions and Stations of the Cross. There was always something to do, thanks to the Church. One was more in touch with life somehow. It's not the same praying in private, you're quite right. It was so different fulfilling one's religious obligations surrounded by ordinary people. These varicose veins . . . (*Looks at her husband.*) To think of all those brash young men who pretend to be atheists, then return to the fold in their old age – well, it's been quite the reverse with you, dear.

AMELIA: It's true, Papa. You never used to miss Mass; you never ate meat on Fridays, and you used to take Communion several times a year. What made you change?

GRANDFATHER: I don't know what you're talking about, my dear.

GRANDMOTHER: Of course you've changed, Pedro. You stopped going to church. And you only went latterly to keep Mamaé and me company. You didn't even kneel at the Elevation. And, whenever we listen to Mass here on the wireless, you don't even bother to cross yourself. Don't you believe in God any more?

GRANDFATHER: Look, I don't know. It's strange . . . but I don't think about it, I don't care.

GRANDMOTHER: Don't you care whether God exists or not? Don't you care if there's an afterlife?

GRANDFATHER: (*Trying to joke*) I must be losing my curiosity in my old age.

GRANDMOTHER: What nonsense you talk, Pedro. A fine consolation it would be if God didn't exist and there was no afterlife.

GRANDFATHER: All right then, God does exist and there is an afterlife. Don't let's argue about something so trivial.

MAMAE: But when it comes to confession he's the best of the lot! (*To* GRANDMOTHER, *who looks at her surprised.*) Father Venancio! What a way he has with words! He captivates you, he hypnotizes you! Father Venancio, I've committed a mortal sin, all because of that Indian woman from Camaná and that damned letter.

(*She puts her hand in front of her mouth, frightened at what*

she has said. She looks at the GRANDPARENTS *and* AMELIA.
*But they are concentrating on their food, as if they hadn't heard
her. However,* BELISARIO *has stopped writing. He looks up
and we can see from his expression that he is profoundly
intrigued.*)

BELISARIO: It's clear that the young lady never had the slightest
doubt about the existence of God, or about the true faith:
it was Catholic, Apostolic and Roman. There's no doubt
she fulfilled her religious obligations with the unerring
simplicity of a star moving around the universe: she went
to church, took Communion, said her prayers, and went
to confession.
(MAMAE, *who has been moving very laboriously over towards*
BELISARIO, *now kneels in front of him as if she is at
confession.*)

MAMAE: Forgive me, Father Venancio, for I have sinned.

BELISARIO: (*Giving her the Benediction*) When was the last time
you came to confession, my child?

MAMAE: A fortnight ago, father.

BELISARIO: Have you offended against God these last two
weeks?

MAMAE: I confess that I gave in to feelings of anger, father.

BELISARIO: How many times?

MAMAE: Twice. The first was last Tuesday. Amelia was cleaning
the bathroom. She was taking her time and I was wanting
to obey a call of nature. I was too ashamed to ask her to
leave. Carmen and Pedro were there and they would have
realized that I wanted to go to the lavatory. So I said as
casually as I could, 'Get a move on with the bathroom,
would you, Amelia.' But she just carried on as if there was
all the time in the world. Well, I was feeling quite
uncomfortable by now, what with the cramp in my
stomach, and I was coming out in a cold sweat. So I
cursed her, mentally of course. But I felt like shouting,
'You confounded idiot! You disagreeable slut! You . . .'

BELISARIO: And the second time, my child?

MAMAE: That treacherous little devil poured away my bottle of
eau-de-Cologne. I'd been given it as a present. The family

is not well off at the moment, father, so for them it was a
lot of money. Amelia and the boys always give me presents
for my birthday and at Christmas, and I depend on them.
I was pleased with that Cologne. It had a lovely smell.
But that little devil opened the bottle and emptied it down
the sink. All because I wouldn't tell him a story, Father
Venancio.

BELISARIO: Was I the treacherous little devil, Mamaé?

MAMAE: Yes, father.

BELISARIO: Did you box my ears? Did you spank me?

MAMAE: I never lay a finger on him. Well, he's not my
grandchild, is he? I'm only an aunt, a sort of second fiddle
in the orchestra. But when I saw that empty Cologne bottle,
father, I was so angry, I locked myself in the bathroom
and stood there in front of the mirror, saying rude words.

BELISARIO: What rude words, my child?

MAMAE: I hardly like to say, Father Venancio.

BELISARIO: That may be so. Now don't be proud.

MAMAE: All right, I'll try, Father. (*Making a big effort*) Bugger
it all! You shit! You shit! You snotty little shit!

BELISARIO: What other sins, my child?

MAMAE: I confess that I lied three times, father.

BELISARIO: Serious lies?

MAMAE: Well sort of, father.

GRANDMOTHER: (*From the table*) What are you talking about,
Elvira?

MAMAE: We've run out of sugar. (*To* BELISARIO) There was a
whole packet, but I hid it. I wanted Carmen to give me
some money. So I told another lie.

GRANDMOTHER: And why should you be going to buy sugar?
Let Amelia go.

MAMAE: No, no. I'll go. I want to take some exercise. (*To*
BELISARIO) It wasn't true, I have great difficulty walking.
My knees ache, and I'm not very steady on my feet.

BELISARIO: And why all those lies, my child?

MAMAE: So I could buy myself a bar of chocolate. I'd been
longing for some for days. That advertisement on the
wireless for Chocolate Sublime made my mouth water.

BELISARIO: Wouldn't it have been easier to ask Grandfather for five *soles*?

MAMAE: He's very hard up at the moment, father. He's living off his sons and they're going through a difficult patch. He makes do with the same razor blade for weeks on end, poor man, sharpening it up for goodness knows how long every morning. It's ages since anyone bought any clothes in the house. We wear what Amelia and the boys hand down to us. How was I going to ask him for money to buy chocolate? So I went to the shop, bought a bar of Sublime, and guzzled it in the street. When I got home, I put the packet of sugar I'd hidden back in the kitchen cupboard. That was the third little piece of deception, father.

BELISARIO: You are too proud, my child.

MAMAE: There's nothing wrong with that. It's not a sin to be proud.

(In the course of the conversation the physical relationship between them has gradually been changing. MAMAE is now in the position she habitually adopts when she tells stories to BELISARIO as a young child.)

BELISARIO: I think it is, Mamaé. Brother Leoncio said the other day in the catechism class that pride was the worst sin of all. That it was Lucifer's favourite.

MAMAE: All right, perhaps it is. But as far as the young lady from Tacna was concerned, it was pride that made her life bearable, you see? It gave her the strength to put up with the disappointments, the loneliness, and all that privation. Without pride she would have suffered a great deal. Besides, it was all she had.

BELISARIO: I don't know why you rate pride so highly. If she loved her fiancé, and he asked her to forgive him for being unfaithful to her with the wicked woman, wouldn't she have been better off just to forgive him and marry him? What use was all this pride to her? After all, she ended up an old spinster, didn't she?

MAMAE: You're very young and you don't understand. Pride is the most important thing a person can have in life. It protects you against everything. Once you lose it, whether

53

you're a man or a woman, the world tramples on you like
an old rag.

BELISARIO: But this isn't a story. It's more like a sermon,
Mamaé. Things have got to happen in stories. And you
never give me nearly enough details. For instance, did the
young lady have any nasty secret habits?

MAMAE: (*Frightened, getting to her feet*) No, of course she didn't.
(*More frightened still*) Nasty . . . what did you say?
(*Horrified*) Nasty what? Nasty whats?

BELISARIO: (*Ashamed*) I said nasty secret thoughts, Mamaé.
Didn't the young lady ever have any nasty secret
thoughts?

MAMAE: (*Sympathetically, as she slips awkwardly back to her
armchair*) You're the one whose head is full of nasty secret
thoughts, my little one.
(*She curls up in her armchair. The* GRANDPARENTS *and*
AMELIA, *unaware of what's happening, carry on eating.*
BELISARIO *has started to write again. He talks as he makes
notes on his papers.*)

BELISARIO: Yes, Mamaé. It's true. I can't help thinking that,
underneath that unworldly façade, behind that serene
expression, there was an infinite source of warmth and
passion which would suddenly well up and make demands
on the young lady. Or was there really nothing else besides
the austere routine of her daily life?
(*He stops writing. He turns to look at* MAMAE. *He addresses
her with a certain pathos.*)
When I was a child, I never imagined you could ever have
been anything other than a little old woman. Even now,
when I try to picture you in your youth, I can't. The young
girl you once were always gives way to the old woman
with the wrinkled face. In spite of all these stories, I'm
still all at sea about the young lady. What happened to
her after she burnt her wedding dress and left the Chilean
officer in the lurch?
(*As* BELISARIO *finishes his speech,* GRANDMOTHER *gets up
from the table and goes over towards* MAMAE.
GRANDFATHER *and* AMELIA *carry on eating, unaware of*

what follows. From time to time GRANDFATHER *throws salt over his food in a sort of frenzy.*)

GRANDMOTHER: Why haven't you packed your suitcases, Elvirita? Pedro wants to leave at dawn so that we arrive at the docks before it gets too hot. We don't want to catch sunstroke, specially you, with that fair skin of yours. (*Pause.*) You know, deep down, I'm glad we're leaving. When my mother died after that dreadful illness, it was almost as if Tacna were starting to die too. And now what with my father's death, I find this town really has quite a disagreeable effect on me. Let's go and pack your suitcases. I'll help you.

MAMAE: I'm not going to Arequipa with you, Carmencita.

GRANDMOTHER: And where are you going to live? Who are you going to stay with in Tacna?

MAMAE: I'm not going to be a burden to you all my life.

GRANDMOTHER: Don't talk nonsense, Elvira. My husband is perfectly happy for you to come with us. You know that. After all, we are practically sisters, aren't we? Well, you'll be a sister to Pedro too. Come on, let's go and pack your suitcases.

MAMAE: Ever since you were married, I've been waiting for this moment. Every night, lying awake, thinking, until morning came with the sound of the bugle at the Chilean barracks. I can't live with you and Pedro. He married you. He didn't bargain for your cousin Elvira as well.

GRANDMOTHER: You're coming to live with us and that's that. There's no more to be said on the subject.

MAMAE: You'd find it a bore in the long run. A whole source of problems. You'd argue because of me. Sooner or later Pedro would throw it back at you that you'd saddled him with a hanger-on for the rest of his life.

GRANDMOTHER: But it won't be for the rest of his life, because soon you'll forget what happened with Joaquín, you'll fall in love and you'll get married. Please, Elvira, we're going to have to get up at crack of dawn. We've got a long journey ahead of us.

BELISARIO: (*Delighted with what he's discovered, jumping up in*

his seat) Long, very tedious and extremely complicated.
Train from Tacna to Arica. Boat from Arica. Then two
days sailing as far as Mollendo. Going ashore there, was
like something out of a circus, wasn't it, Grandma? They
lowered the ladies off the boat into the launch in hampers,
didn't they, Mamaé? Just like cattle. And then there was
that three-day ride across the mountains on horseback to
Arequipa – with the additional hazard of being attacked by
bandits on the way. (*Starts to write enthusiastically.*) Ah,
Belisario, that's what you used to criticize the regionalist
writers so much for: their use of local colour and
extravagant effects.

GRANDMOTHER: Are you afraid of bandits, Elvira? I am, but
at the same time I find them quite delightful. These are
the sort of things you should be thinking about, instead of
all this nonsense.

MAMAE: It's not nonsense, Carmencita.

GRANDMOTHER: You know very well you can't stay in Tacna.
We've nothing left here now. Not even the house – the
new owners are moving in tomorrow.

MAMAE: I'll stay with María Murga.

GRANDMOTHER: That old nanny you once had? Really, Elvira,
the things you come up with!

MAMAE: She's a good-hearted woman. She's offered me a room
in her house, in La Mar. I could share with her youngest
son, my godchild. I'll help out with the housekeeping.
Then there's always my embroidery. I'll make tablecloths,
veils, lace mantillas. And sweets and cakes too. I'll take
them to Máspoli, the confectioner's. That nice Italian will
sell them and give me a commission.

GRANDMOTHER: Like something out of a novelette by Xavier
de Montepin . . . I can just see you living in a Tacna
slum, surrounded by Indians and negroes. You, who are
always so squeamish about everything; you, the finicky
little filly, as father used to call you.

MAMAE: I may be finicky, but I've never felt rich. I'll learn to
live like a pauper, since that's what I am. At least María
Murga's little house is clean.

GRANDMOTHER: Are you going completely out of your mind, Elvira? Stay here and live in La Mar! What's got into you? What's all this about La Mar? First you want to go to Mass there, then it's sunsets you want to look at, and now you're going to live there with María Murga. Has some Negro put a jinx on you? It's getting very late and I'm tired of arguing. I'm going to pack your suitcases and tomorrow Pedro will put you on the Arica train, by force if necessary.

(GRANDMOTHER *goes back to the dining room. She sits down and resumes her meal.*)

MAMAE: What difference does it make whether I stay here or go to María Murga's? Isn't this miserable hole quite as squalid as any shack in La Mar? (*Pause.*) All right, there the people walk about barefoot and we wear shoes. There they all have lice in their hair, as Uncle Menelao keeps reminding us, and we . . . (*Puts her hand up to her head.*) Who knows, that's probably why I'm scratching.

(GRANDFATHER *stands up and goes forward towards* MAMAE. GRANDMOTHER *and* AMELIA *carry on with their meal.*)

GRANDFATHER: Good afternoon, Elvira. I've been looking for you. I'd just like to have a few words with you if I may.

(MAMAE *looks at him for a moment. Then she looks up to heaven as she says:*)

MAMAE: It's so hard to understand you, dear God. You seem to prefer rogues and lunatics to ordinary decent folk. Why, if Pedro was always so fair and so honest, did you give him such a miserable life?

(BELISARIO *gets up from his desk and goes forward towards* MAMAE.)

BELISARIO: Wasn't it a sin for the young lady to reproach God like that, Mamaé? He knows what he's doing and if he gave the gentleman such a hard time, there must have been some good reason for it surely. Perhaps he was going to make up for it by giving him a nice big reward in heaven.

GRANDFATHER: You're like a sister to Carmen, and I think of you as my sister too. You'll never be a stranger in my

57

house. I'm telling you, we're not leaving Tacna without
you.

MAMAE: That may be so, my little one. But the young lady
couldn't understand it. She worked herself up into a fever
thinking, 'Dear God in Heaven, was it because of the
Indian woman in the letter that you put the gentleman
through so much misery? Was it all for that one little
indiscretion that you made the cotton in Camaná get
frosted the very year he was going to get rich?'

BELISARIO: (*Sitting at* MAMAE's *feet, adopting his customary
position while listening to stories*) Had the gentleman
committed a sin? You never told me about that, Mamaé.

GRANDFATHER: I know how much help you've been to Carmen,
both as a friend and a confidante and I'm very grateful to
you. You'll always be part of the family. Do you know I've
left my job at the Casa Gibson? I joined when I was
fifteen, after my father died. I'd like to have been a lawyer,
like him, but it just wasn't possible. Now I'm going to
manage the Saíds' estate in Camaná. We're going to plant
cotton. Who knows? In a few years' time, I might be able
to branch out on my own, buy a little land. Carmen will
have to spend lengthy periods in Arequipa. You'll be able
to keep her company. You see, you won't be a burden in
the house, you'll be an asset.

MAMAE: There was just one little sin, yes, in a life that was
otherwise so pure and noble. But only one, which is
nothing really. And it wasn't the gentleman's fault either
– he was led astray by a depraved woman. The young
lady couldn't understand the injustice of it. (*Looks up to
heaven.*) Was it because of the Indian woman in the letter
that you made the cotton fields in Santa Cruz get blighted
as well? Is that why you made him accept the prefecture
so that he ended up even poorer than he was before?

BELISARIO: But, Mamaé, I know that the young lady was always
worried because he had so much bad luck. But I don't
care about the young lady now. Tell me about the
gentleman. What did he do that was such a sin?

GRANDFATHER: You'll like the house I've rented in Arequipa.

It's in a new district, El Vallecito, beside the river Chilina. You can hear the sound of the water, rippling over the pebbles. And your room looks out over the three volcanoes.

MAMAE: (*Still looking up to heaven*) Was it because of the Indian woman that you stopped him from ever getting another job after leaving the prefecture?

BELISARIO: I'm going to get cross with you, Mamaé. I'm going to throw up my lunch, my dinner and tomorrow's breakfast as well in a minute. To hell with the young lady from Tacna! Tell me about the gentleman! Did he steal something? Did he kill the Indian woman?

GRANDFATHER: It's large, with five bedrooms and a garden where we'll plant trees. Our room and yours are already furnished. But we'll do the others up too for our future family – God willing – with the help of Providence and the Camaná cotton fields. I'm hopeful about my new job, Elvira. The field tests we've done are most encouraging. The cotton plants are thriving – the climate seems to suit them. With determination and a little bit of luck, I'll come out on top, you'll see.

MAMAE: He didn't kill or rob anybody. He let himself be bamboozled by a she-devil. But it wasn't that serious: God wouldn't have had him begging for a job no one would give him, just for that. He wouldn't have had him living on charity when he was still *compos mentis* and in good health.

(*At the beginning of the speech she has been talking to* BELISARIO, *however her mind has started to wander and she now talks to herself.*)

He wouldn't have let him feel like a reprobate and he wouldn't have let him live in such a constant state of anguish that he finally became unhinged and even forgot where he was living . . .

(BELISARIO *stands up and returns to his desk by the proscenium.*)

BELISARIO: (*Writing very quickly*) I'm going to tell you something, Mamaé. The young lady from Tacna was in love with that gentleman. It's quite obvious, although she may not have realized it herself, and it never came out in your stories. But it's certainly going to come out in mine.

GRANDFATHER: I beg you, Elvira. Come and live with us. For ever. Or, rather, for as long as you want. I know it won't be for ever. You're young and attractive, the young men of Arequipa will go crazy about you. Sooner or later, you'll fall for one of them and you'll get married.

MAMAE: (*Getting up*) You're wrong there, Pedro. I'll never marry. But I'm very touched by what you've said. I thank you with all my heart.

(GRANDMOTHER *has got up from the table and goes towards them.*)

GRANDMOTHER: Right, Elvira, your suitcases are all ready. There's just your travelling bag. You'll have to pack it yourself with whatever you want to take by hand. The trunk will go with the rest of the luggage. And please, from now on, stop being so formal with each other. Loosen up a bit. We're all family, after all, aren't we?

(*She makes them embrace each other. The* GRANDPARENTS *lead* MAMAE *towards the table where they each return to their places. They resume the meal. During the conversation between* MAMAE *and the* GRANDPARENTS, BELISARIO *has been writing very enthusiastically, he suddenly stops working, an expression of dismay on his face.*)

BELISARIO: Is this a love story? Weren't you going to write a love story? (*Hits himself on the head.*) You always spoil everything, you keep going off at tangents, Belisario. By the time you get round to writing what you really want to write, you'll be dead. Look, there may be an explanation. (*Noting down*) A writer is someone who writes, not what he wants – that's what the normal person does – but what his demons want him to.

(*He looks at the elderly group of people who carry on eating*) Are you my demons? I owe you everything, yet now that I'm old and you're all dead, you still keep coming to my rescue and helping me out, and so I become even more indebted to you.

(*He gathers his papers together and gets up; he seems impatient and exasperated; he goes towards the dining room where the family carry on eating impassively.*)
Why don't you give me some real help then? Explain things to me, put me in the picture, give me some clarification? Who was that perverse Indian woman who suddenly found her way into the stories about the gentleman and the young lady from Tacna? It must have been someone, there must have been something that touched on a sensitive nerve in the family history, mustn't there, Mamaé? You were obsessed by her, weren't you, Mamaé? She'd been given a thrashing, she was mentioned in some letter or other, and you hated her with such venom that you even used to mix her up with Señora Carlota. (*Walking round the table, shouting*) What happened? What happened? I need to know what happened! I know, the three of you got on marvellously together. But was it like that for all the forty or fifty years you shared under the same roof? Didn't the gentleman ever clasp the young lady surreptitiously by the hand? Did he never make advances to her? Did he never kiss her? Didn't any of those things happen, that normally happen? Or did you control your instincts through the strength of your moral convictions, and quash temptation by sheer force of will? (*By now on his way back to his desk, feeling dejected*) Things like that only happen in stories, Mamaé.
(*While* BELISARIO *is soliloquizing, the doorbell rings.* CESAR *and* AGUSTIN *come in. They kiss the* GRANDPARENTS *and* MAMAE.)

AGUSTIN: How are you feeling, Papá?

GRANDFATHER: I'm fine, absolutely fine, old son.

GRANDMOTHER: No, he's not, Agustín. I don't know what's got into your father, but he gets more and more depressed every day. He walks round the house like some sort of ghost.

AGUSTIN: I'm going to give you some news that'll cheer you up. I had a call from the police and guess what! They've caught the thief.

GRANDFATHER: (*Without knowing what it's all about*) Have they really? Oh good. Good.

AMELIA: The man that attacked you when you were getting off the tram, Papa.

AGUSTIN: And what's more, they've found your watch; it was amongst a whole lot of stolen goods. The man was keeping them in a little cache near Surquillo.

GRANDFATHER: Well, well. That is good news. (*Dubiously, to* GRANDMOTHER) Had they stolen a watch?

CESAR: They identified it by the date engraved on the back: Piura, October 1946.
(*Their voices gradually fade until they are nothing more than a distant murmur.* BELISARIO *stops writing and sits fiddling thoughtfully with his pencil.*)

BELISARIO: Piura, October 1946 . . . There they are, the High Court Judges, presenting him with a watch; and there's Grandfather thanking them for it at that banquet they gave for him at the Club Grau. And there's little Belisario, as pleased as Punch, because he's the Governor's grandson. (*Looks round at his family.*) Was that the final moment of glory? Was it, Grandpa, Grandma, Mama? Was it, Uncle Agustín, Uncle César? Was it, Mamaé? Because after that the calamities fairly started to deluge down on you: no work, no money, bad health and impending dementia. Yet in Piura you looked back nostagically to when you were in Bolivia: there, life had been far better . . . And in Bolivia you looked back to Arequipa: there, life had been far better . . .
(*At the table, the* GRANDPARENTS *carry on chatting with their sons and daughter.*)
Was that the golden age, in Arequipa, when Grandfather used to travel back and forth from Camaná?

GRANDFATHER: (*Youthful, smiling and optimistic*) We've made it at last. We're finally going to reap the rewards after ten whole years of waiting. The cotton is doing marvellously. The plants are larger than we ever dared hope for. The Saíds were in Camaná last week. They brought an expert out from Lima, a string of letters after his name. He was

quite amazed when he saw the cotton fields. He just
couldn't believe it, Carmencita.

GRANDMOTHER: You really do deserve it, Pedro. After all
you've sacrificed, burying yourself away in that wilderness
for so long.

GRANDFATHER: The expert said that if the water doesn't let us
down, and there's no reason why it should, because the
river is higher than ever – we'll have a better harvest this
year than the richest plantations in Ica.

AGUSTIN: Are you going to buy me that doctor's outfit then,
Papa? Because I've changed my mind. I don't want to be
a famous lawyer like Grandfather any more. I am going to
be a famous surgeon.

(GRANDFATHER *nods*.)

CESAR: And you will buy me that scout's uniform, won't you,
Papa?

(GRANDFATHER *nods*.)

AMELIA: (*Sitting on* GRANDFATHER's *knee*) And the chocolate
doll in the window of Ibérica for me, Papakins.

GRANDFATHER: It'll already have been sold by the end of the
harvest, nitwit. But I'll tell you what. I'll have a special
doll made just for you – it'll be the biggest in Arequipa.
(*Pointing to* GRANDMOTHER) And what about this *jolie*
little *laide*? What are we going to give her if the harvest
turns out as we hope?

MAMAE: Can't you think? Hats, of course! Lots and lots of hats!
Large ones, coloured ones, with ribbons and muslin, birds
and flowers.

(*They all laugh.* BELISARIO, *who has started to write, laughs
too as he carries on writing.*)

AMELIA: Why do you like hats so much, Mama?

GRANDMOTHER: They're all the rage in Argentina, dear. Why
do you think I've taken out a subscription with *Para Ti*
and *Leoplán*? I'm putting Arequipa on the map with my
hats. You should wear them too; they'd really do
something for you.

MAMAE: Who knows? You might even land yourself a lawyer.
(*To* GRANDFATHER) If you want a legal genius in the

family, you're going to have to settle for one as a son-in-law, since neither Agustín nor César seem particularly interested in the bar.

AGUSTIN: And what about Mamaé? What are you going to give her if it's a good harvest, Papa?

GRANDFATHER: What's all this about Mamaé? You keep calling Elvira Mamaé. Why?

AMELIA: I'll tell you, Papakins. It's short for Mama Elvira, Mama-é, the E is for Elvira, see? I made it up.

CESAR: Lies, it was my idea.

AGUSTIN: It was mine, you dirty cheats. It was my idea, wasn't it, Mamaé?

GRANDMOTHER: Either call her Mama or Elvira, but not Mamaé – it's so unattractive.

AMELIA: But you're Mama. How can we have two mamas?

AGUSTIN: She can be an honorary Mama then. (*Goes towards* MAMAE.) What do you want Papa to give you after the cotton harvest, Mamaé?

MAMAE: Half a pound of tuppenny rice!

CESAR: Come on, Mamaé, seriously, what would you like?

MAMAE: (*an old woman again*) Some Locumba damsons and a glass of unfermented wine – the kind the Negroes make. (AGUSTIN, CESAR *and* AMELIA, *adults again, all look at each other, intrigued.*)

AGUSTIN: Locumba damsons? Unfermented wine? What are you talking about, Mamaé?

CESAR: Something she'll have heard in one of those radio plays by Pedro Camacho, no doubt.

GRANDMOTHER: Childhood memories, as usual. There were some orchards in Locumba when we were children, and they used to carry baskets full of damsons from them to Tacna. Large, sweet, juicy ones. And there was that muscatel wine. My father used to let us taste it. He'd give us each a teaspoonful – just to try it. There were Negroes working on the plantations then. Mamaé says that when she was born there were still slaves. But there weren't really, were there?

CESAR: You and your fantasies, Mamaé. Like those stories you used to tell us. Now you live them all in your head, don't you, old darling?

AMELIA: (*bitterly*) That's true enough. You're probably responsible for what's happening to my son. All this making him learn poetry by heart, Mamaé.

BELISARIO: (*Putting down his pencil and looking up*) No, that's not true, Mama. It was Grandfather, more like – he was the poetry fanatic. Mamaé only made me learn one. That sonnet, remember? We used to recite it, a verse each. It had been written for the young lady by some long-haired poet, on the back of a mother-of-pearl fan . . . (*Addressing* AGUSTIN) I've got something to tell you, Uncle Agustín. But promise me you'll keep it a secret. Not a word to anyone, mind. And specially not to Mama.

AGUSTIN: Of course not, old son, don't worry. I won't breathe a word, if you don't want me to. What is it?

BELISARIO: I don't want to be a lawyer, Uncle. I loathe all those statutes, and regulations, this law and that law – I loathe all those things we're made to learn at the faculty. I memorize them for the exams, but then I forget them again immediately. They just go in one ear and out the other. I promise you. And I couldn't be a diplomat either, Uncle. I'm sorry, I know it'll come as a disappointment to Mother – and to you, not to mention Grandma and Grandpa. But I can't help it, Uncle, I'm just not cut out for that kind of thing. There's something else. I haven't told anyone about it yet.

AGUSTIN: And what do you think you are cut out for, Belisario?

BELISARIO: I want to be a poet, Uncle.

AGUSTIN: (*Laughs.*) I'm not laughing at you, old son, don't be cross. I'm laughing at myself. I thought you were going to tell me you were a nancy boy. Or that you wanted to go into the priesthood. But a poet, that's altogether less serious. (*Goes back towards the dining room and addresses* AMELIA.) We must face facts, Amelia, Belisario isn't going to pull us out of the mire. Why don't you do as I suggested and send the boy out to work for once in his life?

(BELISARIO *has gone back to the desk and listens to them from there.*)

AMELIA: If things were different, I wouldn't mind him doing whatever he wanted to do. But he's going to die of starvation, Agustín, just like the rest of us. Only he'll be worse off still. A poet, indeed! What sort of a profession is that, I ask you. And I had such high hopes for him. His father would shoot himself all over again, if he knew his only son was turning out to be a poet.

(BELISARIO, *exultant, laughs and mimes shooting himself.*)

MAMAE: Poet? Are you talking about Federico Barreto? Don't let Uncle Menelao hear you. He won't even let his name be mentioned in the house, not since he wrote me that poem.

(MAMAE *smiles at them all, as if they were strangers, bowing politely.* BELISARIO, *leaving his desk, has placed his hands on either side of his forehead so they look like two horns. He starts to charge about, cannoning into the furniture and other objects in the room, including his grandparents, his mother and his two uncles.*)

GRANDMOTHER: Why are you so surprised he wants to be a poet? He takes after his great-grandfather. Pedro's father used to write poetry. And Belisario has always been fairly fanciful, ever since he was so high. Don't you remember in Bolivia with the little nanny goat?

BELISARIO: It's the devil, Grandma. I swear it is. It's on the picture cards, in the Catechism – Brother Leoncio said that he appears in the form of a black billy goat. (*Swearing and kissing his fingers in the form of a cross*) You've got to believe me, Grandma!

AMELIA: But it's not a billy goat, it's only a little nanny goat, dear.

GRANDMOTHER: Besides, it's a present from your grandpa, for Independence Day. Do you really think your grandfather would send us a present of the devil?

BELISARIO: (*Snivelling*) It's Beelzebub, Grandma! It is, it is! You've got to believe me! I swear it is! I did the holy-water test on him. I poured it all over him and he took fright, I promise you.

AGUSTIN: I expect the water wasn't properly blessed, old son.

(BELISARIO *goes over to Mamaé's armchair, weeping.*)

MAMAE: Don't make fun of him, poor little man. I'm listening to you, my precious, come over here.

BELISARIO: (*Affectionately cuddling an imaginary* MAMAE) If only you knew, Mamaé, I still have nightmares about the little nanny goat from Bolivia. She seemed so big. How scared you were of her, Belisario. A billy goat, the devil. Is that what you call a love story?

AMELIA: Why are you so quiet, Papa? Are you feeling ill? Papa, Papa!

GRANDFATHER: (*His head in his hands*) Just a little dizziness, my dear. In my thingumajig. I keep getting it in my thingumajig.

(GRANDMOTHER, CESAR, AGUSTIN, *and* AMELIA *in a great state of alarm all throng round* GRANDFATHER *who has half fainted.*)

CESAR: We must call a doctor! Quick!

AGUSTIN: Wait. Let's take him to his bedroom first.

(*Amid cries of anxiety, all four of them carry* GRANDFATHER *to the inner part of the house.* MAMAE *looks on without moving.*)

MAMAE: (*Looking up to heaven*) Was it because of the Indian woman? Was it because of that youthful little misdemeanour?

(*She gets up with great difficulty. She takes hold of the little wooden chair she uses as a walking aid and, grasping the back, starts out on the slow awkward journey back to her armchair.* BELISARIO, *very serious and resolute now, is waiting for her at the foot of the armchair in the position he habitually adopts for listening to the stories.*)

BELISARIO: Having got so far, I simply have to know now, Mamaé. What was that little misdemeanour?

MAMAE: (*Moving slowly back towards her armchair with some difficulty*) Something dreadful that happened to the young lady, my little one. It was the only time in her entire life. All because of that letter. Because of that wicked woman.

(*Stops to gather strength.*) Poor young lady! They caused her to sin in her thoughts!

BELISARIO: What letter, Mamaé? Tell me the whole story from the beginning.

MAMAE: A letter the gentleman wrote to his wife. His wife was an intimate friend of the young lady from Tacna. They lived together because they were so very fond of each other. They were almost like sisters and that's why, when her friend got married, she took the young lady in to live with her.

BELISARIO: In Arequipa?

(MAMAE *has finally reached her armchair and lets herself fall into it.* BELISARIO *rests his head on her knees.*)

MAMAE: Times were good. It looked as though there was going to be a bumper cotton harvest that year and that the gentleman was going to earn a lot of money and buy a plantation of his own. Because, at that time, the gentleman managed other people's land.

BELISARIO: The plantation in Camaná, the one that belonged to the Saíds. I know all that already. But what about the letter, Mamaé, what about the Indian woman?

(GRANDFATHER *appears at the back of the stage. He sits down. Enter* SEÑORA CARLOTA, *with a broom and a feather duster. She is dressed as in the first act, only here she appears to be carrying out the duties of a servant girl. As she sweeps and dusts, she moves back and forth in front of* GRANDFATHER, *suggestively.* GRANDFATHER, *despite himself, starts to follow her with his gaze.*)

MAMAE: Camaná was in the back of beyond. A little village without roads or even a church. The gentleman wouldn't allow his wife to bury herself in a wasteland like that. So he left her in Arequipa, with the young lady, so she could have some sort of social life. He had to spend months away from his family. But he was a very good man; he had always treated the labourers and servants at the plantation with the utmost consideration. Until one day . . .

GRANDFATHER: (*Reciting*) 'My beloved wife, my treasure: I write to you, my soul worn to tatters with remorse. On

68

our wedding night we made an oath of undying love and
fidelity. We swore we'd be totally frank with each other.
These last five years, I've kept scrupulously to that oath,
as I know you have too, you saint among saints.'
(SEÑORA CARLOTA, *emboldened by the looks* GRANDFATHER
*is giving her, takes off her blouse, as if it were very hot. The
brassière she is wearing underneath barely covers her breasts.*)

BELISARIO: (*With restrained anguish*) Was it a letter the
gentleman wrote to the young lady?

MAMAE: No, to his wife. The letter arrived in Arequipa, and
when the gentleman's wife read it, she turned as white as
snow. The young lady had to give her valerian drops and
sponge her brow. Then the gentleman's wife shut herself
up in her room and the young lady heard her weeping with
sighs that rent the soul. Her curiosity was too great for
her. So that afternoon, she searched the room. And do you
know where the letter was? It was hidden inside a hat.
Because the gentleman's wife loved hats. And, unluckily
for her, the young lady read it.
(GRANDFATHER *stretches out his hand and takes hold of*
SEÑORA CARLOTA, *as she brushes past him. She pretends to
be surprised and get annoyed, but after a brief, silent struggle,
she gives in to him.* GRANDFATHER *sits her on his knees,
caresses her, as he continues to recite the letter.*)

GRANDFATHER: 'I'd sooner cause you pain than lie to you, my
love. I could never live at peace in the knowledge that I'd
deceived you. Yesterday, for the first time in five years, I
was unfaithful to you. Forgive me, I beg you, on my
bended knee. It was too strong for me. I was overwhelmed
by an emotion which swept away all my principles, all
my vows, like a hurricane rooting up everything in its path.
I have decided to tell you this, although you may curse
me. Your absence is to blame. Dreaming of you at night,
here in Camaná, has been nothing but a torture to me,
and still is. My blood starts to race at the very thought of
you. I'm beset by notions of abandoning everything,
jumping on my horse and galloping to Arequipa, to your

side, where I can hold your beautiful body in my arms
again, and carry you to the bedroom . . .'
(*His voice slowly fades away.*)

MAMAE: The young lady suddenly felt as if everything was
starting to go round. The bathroom, where she was reading
the letter, seemed to be turning into an enormous top that
spun round and round – the house, Arequipa, the whole
world became a giant wheel off which the young lady was
falling, falling . . . as if from a precipice. She thought her
heart and her head were going to burst. And her face was
burning with shame.

BELISARIO: (*Very seriously*) Did she feel ashamed because she'd
read about the gentleman beating a servant girl?
(GRANDFATHER *and* SEÑORA CARLOTA *have now slid on to
the floor.*)

MAMAE: (*Shaking*) Yes, she did, very. She couldn't imagine
how the gentleman could so much as lay a finger on a
woman. Not even a perverse Indian.

BELISARIO: (*Very moved*) Had she never read any novels in
which men beat women?

MAMAE: She was a well brought-up young lady and there were
certain things she did not read, my little one. But this
was worse than reading about them in a book, because she
knew the author of the letter. She read it over and over
again, but still she couldn't believe that the gentleman
would have done such a thing.

GRANDFATHER: 'Her name is not important. She was beneath
contempt, one of those Indians who clean out hostels, a
mere animal, an object almost. I wasn't blinded by her
charms, Carmen. It was you, the memory of you, your
charms, your body – that was the reason for my nostalgia.
Thinking about you, longing for you, that was what made
me give in to such madness and make love to the Indian
woman. On the floor, like a beast. Yes, you must know
everything.'

BELISARIO: (*Also trembling, now pronouncing the words as if they
were burning him*) So the gentleman's wife went as white
as snow, all because of a few lashes he happened to give

70

the servant. Is that why the young lady felt the world was
coming to an end? You're not hiding anything from me,
are you? The gentleman didn't by any chance go too far,
did he, and do the Indian woman in, Mamaé?

MAMAE: Suddenly, the young lady started to feel something
else. Something worse than dizziness. Her whole body
started to shake and she had to sit down on the bath. The
letter was so very explicit that she felt as if she were
receiving the thrashing that the gentleman gave the wicked
woman.

GRANDFATHER: 'And there in my arms, the little whelp lay
whimpering with pleasure. But it wasn't her I was making
love to. It was you, my angel. Because I had my eyes
closed, it was you I was seeing – and it wasn't her smell,
it was yours, that sweet rose-scented fragrance of your skin
which intoxicated me so . . .'

BELISARIO: But in what way did that letter make the young
lady sin in her thoughts, Mamaé?

MAMAE: (*Distraught*) She imagined that instead of thrashing
Señora Carlota, the gentleman was thrashing her.

GRANDFATHER: 'When it was all over and I opened my eyes,
it wasn't you I was looking at with your drowsy blue eyes,
but that unfamiliar face with its coarse strange features . . .
That was my punishment. Forgive me, forgive me, I
know I've been weak, but it was all because of you,
thinking about you, wanting you, that I finally failed you.

BELISARIO: So the young lady imagined that the gentleman was
thrashing her. Where's the sin in that? That wasn't a sin,
Mamaé. That was plain stupidity. And anyway, which
Señora Carlota are you talking about? I thought she was
the wicked woman from Tacna?

MAMAE: Of course it was a sin. Isn't it a sin to hurt your
neighbour? If the young lady fancied the gentleman was
ill-treating her, then she must have wanted the gentleman
to offend against God. Don't you realize?

(GRANDFATHER *gets up. With a gesture of disgust he dismisses*
SEÑORA CARLOTA, *who goes away, casting a sardonic glance*

at MAMAE. GRANDFATHER *passes his hand over his face,*
straightens his clothes.)

GRANDFATHER: 'When I come to Arequipa, I'll throw myself
at your feet until you forgive me. I'll demand from you a
penance even harsher than my sin. Be generous, be
understanding, my angel. I love you and adore you and
want to kiss you more than ever. Your ever loving husband,
Pedro.'

(*He goes out.*)

MAMAE: That evil thought was her punishment for reading
other people's letters. So be warned. Never pry into what
doesn't concern you.

BELISARIO: There are things that don't make sense. Why did
the gentleman beat the Indian woman? You said it was
she who was the perverse one and he was goodness itself,
and yet in the story he gives her a thrashing. Whatever
had she done?

MAMAE: It must have been something dreadful for the poor
gentleman to fly off the handle the way he did. She must
have been one of those women who talk about passion and
pleasure and nasty things like that.

BELISARIO: Did the young lady of Tacna go and confess her
evil thoughts?

MAMAE: The terrible thing is, Father Venancio, as I was reading
that letter I felt something I can't explain. A sort of
elation, an inquisitiveness, which made my whole body
tingle. Then suddenly, envy for the victim of what was
described in the letter. I had evil thoughts, father.

BELISARIO: The Devil is always on the lookout – he never
misses an opportunity to tempt Eve, like in the
beginning . . .

MAMAE: It had never happened to me before, father. I'd had a
few warped ideas, vengeful feelings, I'd been envious and
angry. But I'd never had thoughts like this before! Least
of all about someone I respect so much. The master of
the house I live in, my cousin's husband, the very person
who gave me a home. Ahhh! Ahhh!

BELISARIO: (*Getting up, going towards his desk, starting to write*)
Look, young lady from Tacna, I'm going to give you
Brother Leoncio's remedy for evil thoughts. The moment
they strike, go down on your knees, wherever you are,
and ask the Virgin for help. Out loud, if necessary.
(*Imitating Brother Leoncio*) 'Mary, keep temptation away,
like water keeps a cat at bay.'
(BELISARIO *carries on writing.*)

MAMAE: (*To an imaginary* BELISARIO *still at her feet*) When your
Grandma Carmen and I were children together in Tacna,
we went through a phase of being very pious. We did
penances severer than the ones imposed at confessional.
And when your Grandmother Carmen's mother – my aunt
Amelia – fell ill, we made a vow, so that God would save
her. Do you know what it was? To have a cold bath each
day. (*Laughs.*) At that time, it was considered madness
to have a bath every day. That habit came in later when
the foreigners arrived. It was quite a performance. The
servants heated up pails of water, the doors and windows
were all bolted, the bath was spiced with salts, and when
you got out of the tub, you went straight to bed so you
didn't catch your death of cold. So in our efforts to save
Aunt Amelia, we were ahead of our time. Every morning
for a whole month, we got up as quietly as mice and
plunged into icy cold water. We'd come out, our skin all
covered in goosepimples, and our lips purple. Aunt
Amelia recovered and we believed that it was all because
of that vow we made. But a couple of years later she fell
ill again and was in the most agonizing pain for months on
end. She finally went out of her mind with all the
suffering. It's hard sometimes to understand God, my little
one. Take your Grandpa Pedro, for example. Was it fair
that everything should have turned out so badly for him,
when he'd always been so upright and so good?
(BELISARIO *stops writing and looks up.*)

BELISARIO: And, you, Mamaé? Why didn't everything turn out
well for you in life? What youthful little misdemeanour

were you punished for? Was it for reading that letter? Did
the young lady from Tacna read that letter? Did that
letter actually exist?

(MAMAE *has taken from among her old clothes, an exquisite
mother-of-pearl fan, dating from the beginning of the century.
After fanning herself for a moment, she lifts it up towards her
eyes, and reads something that is written on it. She looks
apprehensively to right and left in case anyone is listening to
her. She is going to recite, in a voice full of emotion, the poem
on the fan, when* BELISARIO *gets in ahead of her and says the
first line.*)

BELISARIO: 'There's none more beautiful than thee, Elvira . . .'
MAMAE: (*Continuing reciting*) 'Standing here before thee, oft I
wonder . . .'
BELISARIO: 'Art thou angel? Art thou goddess?'
MAMAE: 'Thou'rt so modest, virtuous, sweet and humble . . .'
BELISARIO: 'Fortune smile upon thee, sweet deserver . . .'
MAMAE: 'A thousand times more fortunate be he . . .'
BELISARIO: 'Who finally may call thee wife.'
MAMAE: 'For I am but a humble bard of Tacna . . .'
BELISARIO: 'Who with heavy heart doth end my weary life . . .'
MAMAE: 'And deem myself too small for such an honour.'
BELISARIO: 'Mistrust me, therefore, not, when I thee flatter:'
MAMAE: 'Since I cannot, sweet Elvira, be thy master . . .'
BELISARIO: 'Let me, leastwise, be thy servant and thy slave.'

(*He starts to write again. As he says the last line of the poem*
AMELIA *enters from the inner part of the house, sobbing. She
leans against a chair, dries her eyes.* MAMAE *remains in her
chair, as if asleep, only her eyes are open – a melancholy
smile fixed on her face.* CESAR *enters from the inner part of the
house, an expression of remorse on his face.*)

AMELIA: She's dead, isn't she?

(CESAR *nods and* AMELIA *leans her head on his shoulder and
cries. He lets out a little sob too. Enter* AGUSTIN, *also from
the inner part of the house.*)

AGUSTIN: Come on, cheer up. It's Mama we ought to be
thinking about now. It's particularly dreadful for her.

CESAR: We'll have to put her on tranquillizers until she's got over the shock.

AMELIA: I feel so miserable, César.

CESAR: It's as if the whole family were falling apart . . .

BELISARIO: (*Looking towards the audience*) Has Mamaé died?

AGUSTIN: She got weaker and weaker until finally, like a little flame, she flickered out altogether. First it was her hearing, then her legs, her hands, her bones. Today it was her heart.

BELISARIO: (*Still in the same position*) Mother, is it true that Mamaé's died?

AMELIA: Yes, dear, it is. She's gone away to heaven, the poor darling.

CESAR: But you're not going to cry, Belisario, are you?

BELISARIO: (*Crying*) Of course I'm not. Why should I? We all have to die sometime, don't we, Uncle César? Men don't cry, do they, Uncle Agustín?

CESAR: Choke back those tears, son, and let's see you behave like a brave little man, eh?

BELISARIO: (*Still at his desk, facing the audience*) Like that famous lawyer I am going to be one day, uncle?
(*Making an effort to stifle the emotion that has got the better of him,* BELISARIO *starts to write again.*)

AMELIA: That's right, like the famous lawyer you're going to be one day.

AGUSTIN: Go and join Mama, Amelia. We've got to talk about the funeral arrangements.
(AMELIA *nods and goes out, towards the inner part of the house.* AGUSTIN *moves towards* CESAR.)
And funerals, as you know, cost money. We'll give her the simplest there is. But even so: it still costs money.

CESAR: All right, Agustín. I'll do what I can. I am more hard up than you are. But I'll help you out all the same.

AGUSTIN: It's not me you're helping, but Mamaé. After all, she was as much your Mamaé as she was mine. You'll also have to help me with the legal proceedings, that trying district council, the cemetery and so on . . .
(CESAR *and* AGUSTIN *go out towards the street.* MAMAE

remains still, huddled in her armchair. BELISARIO *has just finished writing. On his face we can detect a mixture of feelings: satisfaction, certainly, for having completed what he wanted to relate, and at the same time emptiness and nostalgia for something which is over, which he has lost.*)

BELISARIO: It's not a love story, it's not a romantic story. So what is it, then? (*Shrugs his shoulders.*) You'll never cease marvelling at the strange way stories are born, will you, Belisario? They get embellished with things one believes to be long forgotten – the most unlikely events are retrieved from the memory only to be distorted by the imagination. (*Looks at* MAMAE.) My only recollections of you were that final image: a shadow of a woman, huddled up in her armchair, who wet her knickers. (*Gets up and goes towards* MAMAE.) You were very good to me, Mamaé. Of course you were. But you had no alternative, had you? Why did it occur to me to write your story? Well, you should know that instead of becoming a lawyer, a diplomat or a poet, I ended up by devoting myself to a craft I probably learnt from you: that of telling stories. Yes, that may be the reason: to pay off a debt. As I didn't know the real story, I've had to add to the things I remembered, bits which I made up or borrowed from here and there. Like you did in your stories about the young lady from Tacna, didn't you, Mamaé?

(*He closes her eyes and kisses her on the forehead. As he moves away towards one of the wings, the curtain falls.*)

KATHIE AND THE HIPPOPOTAMUS

A Comedy in Two Acts

To Norma Aleandro

INTRODUCTION

Theatre as fiction

In a make-believe Paris, a man and a woman agree to meet for two hours each day to devote themselves to fiction – to the art of telling lies. For her, it is a hobby; for him, a job. But lies are seldom either gratuitous or innocuous; they are nurtured by our unfulfilled desires and our failures and are as accurate an indication of our characters as all those irrefutable words of truth we utter.

To lie is to invent; it is to add to real life another fictitious one disguised as reality. Morally abhorrent when practised in everyday life, this strategem seems quite acceptable, even praiseworthy when practised under the pretext of art. We applaud the novelist, artist or dramatist who, through his skill at handling words, images or dialogue, persuades us that these contrivances which set out merely to be a reflection of life are in fact life itself. But are they? Fiction is the life that wasn't, the life we'd liked to have had but didn't, the life we'd rather not have had or the one we'd like to relive, without which the life we are actually leading seems incomplete. Because unlike animals, who live out their lives to their full potential from beginning to end, we are only able to realize a small part of ours.

Our hunger for life and our expectations always far exceed our capacity as human beings who have been granted the perverse privilege of being able to dream up a thousand and one adventures while only being capable of realizing ten, at the most. The inevitable gulf between the concrete reality of our human existence and those desires and aspirations which exacerbate it which can never themselves be satisfied, is not merely the origin of man's unhappiness, dissatisfaction and rebelliousness. It is also the *raison d'être* of fiction, a deceptive device through which we can compensate artificially for the inadequacies of life, broaden the asphyxiatingly narrow confines of our condition, and gain access to worlds that are richer, sometimes shabbier, often more intense, but always different

from the one fate has provided us with. Thanks to the conceits
of fiction, we can augment our experience of life – one man may
become many different men, a coward may become a hero, a
sluggard a man of action, and a virgin a prostitute. Thanks to
fiction we discover not only what we are, but also what we are
not and what we'd like to be. The lies of fiction enrich our lives
by imbuing them with something they'll never actually have,
but once their spell is broken, we are left helpless and
defenceless, brutally aware of the unbridgeable gap between
reality and fantasy. For the man who doesn't despair, who
despite everything is prepared to throw himself in at the deep
end, fiction is there waiting for him, its arms laden with
illusions, which have matured out of the leavening of our own
sense of emptiness: 'Come in, come in, come and play a game
of lies.' But sooner or later we discover, like Kathie and
Santiago in their 'little Parisian attic', that we're really playing
a melancholy little game of deception, in which we assume
those roles we long to play in real life or, alternatively, a
terrifying game of truth, which in real life we'd do anything
to avoid.

Theatre isn't life, but make-believe, that is to say another
life, a life of fiction, a life of lies. No genre demonstrates as
splendidly as theatre the equivocal nature of art. The characters
we see on stage, as opposed to the ones we find in novels or
paintings, are flesh and blood and act out their roles right in
front of us. We watch them suffer, enjoy themselves, laugh, get
angry. If the show succeeds, we become totally convinced of
their authenticity by the way they speak, move, gesture and
emote. Are we in fact aware of any difference between them
and real life? Not at all, except that we know they are a
pretence, a fiction, that they are theatre. Curiously enough, in
spite of its blatantly deceptive and fraudulent nature, there
have always been (and always will be) those who insist that
theatre – and fiction in general – should express and propagate
religious, ideological, historical and moral truths. But I don't
agree. The role of the theatre – of fiction in general – is to
create illusions, to deceive.

Fiction is not a reproduction of life: it complements it by

cutting down on what we have enough of in real life, and adding what is lacking, by bringing order and logic to what we experience as chaotic and absurd, or alternatively injecting an element of mystery, craziness and risk into the balanced, the routine, and the secure. There is evidence of this systematic modification of life throughout the history of humanity: it has been recorded rather like the negative of a photograph – in the long catalogue of adventures, passions, gestures, infamies, manners, excesses, subtleties, which man had to invent because he was incapable of living them himself.

Dreaming, creating works of fiction (the same as reading, going to plays, suspending disbelief) is an oblique way of protesting against the mediocrity of life and it is also an effective, if cursory way of ridiculing it. Fiction, when we find ourselves under its spell, bewitched by its artifice, makes us feel complete, by transforming us momentarily into those great villains, those angelic saints, or those transparent idiots, which we are constantly being incited to become by our desires and aspirations, our cowardice, our inquisitiveness or simply our spirit of contradiction, and when it returns us to our normal state, we find we have changed, that we are more aware of our limitations, more eager for fantasy and less ready to accept the status quo.

This is what happens to the main characters in *Kathie and the Hippopotamus*, the banker's wife and the writer in the little attic room where the play is set. When I wrote it, I didn't even know that its underlying theme was the relationship between life and art; this particular alchemy fascinates me because the more I practise it the less I understand it. My intention was to write a farce, by pushing the characters to the point of unreality (but not beyond because total unreality is boring), taking as a starting point a situation that had been haunting me for some time: a lady employs a writer to help her compose an adventure story. She is, at this point, a pathetic creature in so far as art for her seems to be a last resort against a life of failure; he is unable to come to terms with the fact that he wasn't Victor Hugo whose abundant personality he admires in all its many aspects: the romantic, the literary, the political, and the sexual. During their working sessions and arising from the transformations the story itself undergoes between what Kathie dictates and what her amanuensis writes down, their respective lives, both the real and imaginary sides of them, that is, what they actually were and what they would have liked to have been – are acted out on stage, summoned together by memory, desire, fantasy, association and chance. At some point during my work on the play, I noticed beside the ghosts of Kathie and Santiago, who I was trying to breathe life into, other little ghosts queuing up behind them, waiting to earn their rightful place in the play. Now when I discover them, I recognize them, and am once again quite astounded. Santiago's and Kathie's fantasies, quite apart from their real lives, in many ways reveal my own, and the same is no doubt true of anyone who puts on display that crude mass of raw material out of which he fashions his fiction.

Mario Vargas Llosa

CHARACTERS

KATHIE KENNETY
SANTIAGO ZAVALA
ANA DE ZAVALA
JUAN

The action takes place some time in the 1960s in Kathie Kennety's 'Parisian attic'.

SET, COSTUME, EFFECTS

Kathie Kennety's 'little Parisian attic' is not a caricature: it has that air of permanence and authenticity about it as if it were a real place.

Kathie, a woman with a sense of taste, has furnished her 'studio' in an attractive manner, reminiscent of the sort of artist's garret one finds in pictures, novels, postcards and films; it also has something of the genuine *chambres de bonne* where students and impoverished foreigners congregate on the left bank of the Seine.

Under the sloping ceiling, there are ageing beams; on the walls, posters of the ubiquitous Eiffel Tower, the inevitable Arc de Triomphe, the Louvre, some Impressionist paintings, a Picasso, and – one essential detail – a portrait or bust of Victor Hugo. There is nothing of great elegance, nothing superfluous, just what is necessary to give an impression of comfort and warmth: a little retreat where the occupant can feel safe and protected from the turmoil and scrutiny of the outside world, free to conjure up her innermost demons and confront them face to face. There is a thick wooden desk, a broad delapidated sofa, covered all over with rugs, some cushions on the floor, the tape-recorder and the typewriter, a small record-placer, the usual records of Juliette Greco, Léo Ferré, Yves Montand, Georges Brassens, etc. Filing cabinets, notebooks, papers and some books, but not too many, because Kathie's idea of culture has little to do with literature.

There is nothing special or unusual about what Kathie or Santiago wear. The story takes place some time in the 1960s and this can be indicated in the way they dress. Santiago's clothes reflect the modest salary and the hectic life of a journalist and lecturer, and it would not be inappropriate for Kathie to dress, when she's in her little attic, in the Bohemian style of Saint-Germain in the 1950s: black turtle-neck jersey, tight-fitting trousers, stiletto-heeled boots. The costumes Ana and Juan wear need not be so precise. Unlike Kathie and Santiago, who are characters of flesh and blood, contemporaneous with the action, they only live in the minds and the imaginations of the two protagonists. They exist in so far as they are projections of the protagonists' memories and fantasies. Their subjective, if not to say perceptual, nature should perhaps be subtly suggested in the way they dress, but any outlandishness or exaggeration should be avoided. One possibility is that, as Ana's and Juan's thought-processes, gestures, speech and names fluctuate in accordance with Kathie's and Santiago's recollections, so might their dress, if only in small details – such as the acquisition of a hat, a cloak, a pair of spectacles, or a wig – to emphasize the metaphorical, volatile nature of their personalities. The same might happen with Kathie and Santiago when they shed their identities and assume new ones, as a projection of either their own or the other's fantasy. But none of this should be carried beyond the bounds of credibility; the characters should never seem grotesque or like circus clowns – *Kathie and the Hippopotamus* is not a farce, and should not be performed as such. It is in the subtext, the inner workings of the characters' minds lying at the root of what they say and do on stage, that we find elements of farce.

The action of the play exceeds the conventional limits of normal life: it takes place not only in the objective world but also in the subjective world of the characters themselves, as if there were no dividing line between the two, and it moves with complete freedom from one to the other. Any exaggerated speech, gesture or movement, any distortion of reality such as we find in slapstick comedy would be counterproductive and out of place here: the play's intention is not to provoke laughter through any crude stylization of human experience, but, by using the combined techniques of humour, suspense and melodrama, to lead the audience imperceptibly to accept this integration of the visible with the invisible, of fact with fantasy, of present with past, as a separate reality. Objective life becomes suffused with subjectivity, while the subjective life of the individual acquires the physical and temporal tangibility of objective reality. Characters of flesh and blood become to a certain extent creatures of fantasy, while the phantoms that emerge from their imaginations become creatures of flesh and blood. The deepest concerns of *Kathie and the Hippopotamus* are, perhaps, the nature of theatre in particular and fiction in general: not only that which is written and read, but, more importantly, that which human beings practise unwittingly in their everyday lives.

Visual effects can be helpful in the staging of the play, but it is primarily the use of music as a background presence that can evoke most effectively the different atmospheres – Paris, Black Africa, and the Arab world – that is to say the exotic appeal of a good part of the story.

It may not be superfluous to add that in this play I have tried, as I have in my novels, to create an illusion of totality – which should be understood qualitatively rather than quantitatively in this case. The play does not attempt to paint a broad panorama of human experience but seeks to illustrate that experience itself is both objective and subjective, real and imaginary, and that life is made up of both these levels. Man talks, acts, dreams and invents. Life is not just a rational catalogue of events – fantasy and ambition play their part as well. It is not the result of cold planning – but also of spontaneity. Although these two aspects of human experience are not entirely interdependent, neither could do without its counterpart without destroying itself. For a long time we have resorted to fantasy as an escape from reality when it becomes unbearable for us, but this is not just escapism; it is a devious means of gaining the knowledge required for understanding that reality. If we could not distance ourselves from it, it would seem confused and chaotic, little more than a stifling routine. The exploits of the imagination enrich reality and help us better our lives. If we didn't dream, life would seem irredeemable; if we didn't allow our imaginations free rein, the world would never change.

Mario Vargas Llosa

This translation of *Kathie and the Hippopotamus* was first performed as a rehearsed reading on 15 April 1989 at the Gate Theatre, Notting Hill. The cast was as follows:

KATHIE KENNETY	Marian Diamond
SANTIAGO ZAVALA	Thomas Wheatley
ANA DE ZAVALA	Geraldine Fitzgerald
JUAN	Alan Barker
Director	David Graham-Young

Life, such as it has been made for men, can only be born with lies.

Simone Weil, 'Miscellaneous Thoughts about Loving God'

> Go, go, go, said the bird: human kind
> Cannot bear very much reality.

T. S. Eliot, *Four Quartets*

ACT ONE

When the curtain goes up, Parisian music from the 1940s or 1950s can be heard in the background. SANTIAGO *is dictating into a tape-recorder.* KATHIE *walks round him, going through some notes, recalling her experiences. When their voices become audible, the background music fades into an Arab melody with flutes, hornpipes and drums.*

KATHIE: I stood beside the Sphinx until it got dark – then suddenly the lights came on.

SANTIAGO: Oblivious of the advancing night I stand transfixed, gazing up at the Sphinx. All at once, an unearthly glow illuminates her face, and she smiles serenely down at me. There we confront each other – I, the woman of flesh and blood; she with her heart of stone, head aloft, and lion's claws.

KATHIE: There were masses of stars. It was late and I felt – I don't know – sort of alone out there amongst all those Egyptian tombs.

SANTIAGO: I meander midst vast pyramidical sepulchres and megalithic colossi of the ancient pharaohs: beneath the canopy of night, an infinity of stars, which floats over Cairo in an indigo sea of opalescent hues.

KATHIE: It was rash of me to have stayed behind. Who would there be to defend me in case of danger? But then I remembered my revolver and didn't feel afraid any more.

SANTIAGO: Not a living soul in sight – neither man, nor beast, nor plant: hardly aware of my isolation, I muse on that far-off civilization that raised such memorials, a race so perfectly attuned to the supernatural, as fish are to the ocean. I hold silent communion with the Sphinx. Suddenly my illusion is shattered and harsh reality reasserts itself: what am I doing there, alone, exposing myself to a thousand perils – does a hunger-crazed jackal or some ruthless desperado lie in wait? But I am reassured as I remember my small revolver with its mother-of-pearl

handle which accompanies me round the world like a
faithful dog.

KATHIE: At that point, the man appeared in front of me. Heaven
knows how he'd got there. I couldn't even shout, I was
so frightened. What was he going to do to me?
(*Enter* JUAN.)

SANTIAGO: The figure of a man, in a red cape and white turban,
suddenly emerges in front of me, as if conjured from the
hot desert air or out of the past. He is tall, slim, with pitch-
black eyes and gleaming white teeth. Is he going to attack
me? Is he going to violate me? Should I run for help, burst
into tears?

KATHIE: (*Addressing herself for the first time to* SANTIAGO) I don't
like that last bit.

SANTIAGO: We'll rub it out then. Where shall we go back to?

KATHIE: To where the man appears in front of me.
(SANTIAGO *leans over his tape-recorder to rub out the last part
of his dictation.* JUAN *moves closer to* KATHIE. *They both
undergo a transformation: they are now like two youngsters
chatting on the corner of the street.*)

JUAN: 'Man'? You mean, of course, 'boyfriend'.

KATHIE: You, my boyfriend? Ha ha, excuse me while I laugh.

JUAN: I'll excuse you anything you like, Kathie. Except one
thing – don't try and pretend you're not in love with me.

KATHIE: But I'm not.

JUAN: You will be though.

KATHIE: Don't you ever get tired of me saying no to you,
Johnny?

JUAN: Once I get an idea into my head, there's no stopping
me, Pussikins. I'll keep on proposing to you till you say
yes to me. You'll be my girlfriend, my fiancée, and we'll
end up getting married, want to bet?

KATHIE: (*dying of laughter*) So I'm going to get married to you
now, am I?

JUAN: And who else are you going to marry, if you don't marry
me?

KATHIE: I've plenty of admirers, Johnny.

JUAN: You'll pick the best though.

KATHIE: How conceited you are.

JUAN: I know very well who's been proposing to you. And why, may I ask, did you send them all packing? Because you're really nuts about me.

KATHIE: You're so conceited, Johnny.

JUAN: I've every reason to be conceited. Do you want me to tell you why?

KATHIE: Yes, go on, tell me why.

JUAN: Am I or am I not better than Bepo Torres?

KATHIE: How are you better than Bepo Torres?

JUAN: I surf better than him for a start. He can't even stand on the board. Besides, I'm better looking than he is.

KATHIE: You think you're the best-looking man around, don't you?

JUAN: Well, I'm better-looking than Bepo Torres anyway. And Kike Ricketts. Do you really think Kike's a match for me? Does he surf better than me? Is he better-looking than me?

KATHIE: He's a better dancer than you.

JUAN: Kike? Ha ha, excuse me while I laugh. Can he do the mambo better than me? (*Does a few steps.*) The cha-cha-cha? (*Another few steps.*) The huaracha? (*Another few steps.*) When I dance at parties, everyone gathers round, as you very well know. Who showed poor old Kike how to dance in the first place? I even showed him how to smooch.

KATHIE: He's better at the marinera and the creole waltz than you are.

JUAN: The marinera! The creole waltz! I say, how frightfully refined. No one does those fuddy-duddy dances these days, Pussikins.

KATHIE: You're just dying of jealousy, aren't you? You're jealous of Bepo, of Kike, of Gordo . . .

JUAN: Gordo? Me, jealous of Gordo Rivarola? What's Gordo got that I haven't? A chevrolet convertible nineteen fifty. Well, I've got a Studebaker convertible nineteen fifty-one. Do me a favour, Pussikins, please. Why should I be jealous of Bepo, or Kike, or Gordo, or Sapo Saldívar, or Harry Santana, or Abel, my brother, or any of the rest of them who have proposed to you for that matter? They aren't even in the same league as me, any of them, and you know it . . .

KATHIE: (*Reflectively – forgetting about* JUAN, *and emerging for a moment from her fantasy world*) Kike, Bepo, Harry, Gordo Rivarola . . . It seems ages ago now . . .

JUAN: (*Who hasn't been listening to her*) And then there's another reason, of course. Shall I be quite frank with you? Shall I?

KATHIE: (*Returning to her fantasy world*) Yes, Johnny. Be quite frank with me.

JUAN: I've got money, Pussikins.

KATHIE: Do you really think that matters to me? My daddy's got more money than your daddy, silly.

JUAN: Exactly, Pussikins. With me you can be sure it's you I want – if I marry you it'll be for no other reason but yourself. You can't be so sure about that with the others, can you? I heard my old man saying to yours only yesterday: 'Be careful of those young men who gad about with your daughter. They're out to land the best deal of their lives.'

KATHIE: (*Confused*) Don't be so vulgar, Johnny.

JUAN: (*Confused also*) I'm not being vulgar. Marrying for money's not being vulgar. OK, if I was, I apologize. You see, you've gone all quiet. It's true what I'm telling you, ask your old man. You couldn't deny it. You see, I'm already starting to convince you. Next time I propose to you, I don't think you'll send me packing quite so quickly, eh, Pussikins . . .

(*As his voice fades,* KATHIE *distances herself from him, physically and mentally.* JUAN *remains on stage. He is like a little boy; he saunters about, whistling, looking idly around with his hands in his pockets.* SANTIAGO *has finished erasing the last part of the dictation on the tape-recorder.*)

SANTIAGO: Ready, it's all rubbed out. Shall we carry on from your visit to the Sphinx or shall we go on to another chapter, señora?

KATHIE: Why don't you call me Kathie? 'Señora' makes me feel so old.

SANTIAGO: Can I ask you a question? Where did 'Kathie Kennety' come from?

KATHIE: Don't you like the name?

SANTIAGO: It's pretty. But how did it originate? Why did you choose it?

KATHIE: If I used my real name, no one would take my book seriously. Peruvian names don't somehow seem right for authors. 'Kathie Kennety', on the other hand, has a certain exotic, musical, cosmopolitan ring to it. (*Looks at him reflectively.*) Santiago Zavala doesn't sound too good either, not for an artist. Why don't you change it? Yes, yes, let me rechristen you. Let's see now . . . I know. Mark. Mark Griffin. May I call you that? We'll only use it here, in this little attic. You don't mind?

SANTIAGO: No, señora, I don't mind.

KATHIE: Do you really find me so old, you can't call me Kathie?

SANTIAGO: Of course not. But I've got to get used to the idea. I'm working for you, remember. I think of you as my boss.

KATHIE: Why not think of me as a colleague? Come on, we mustn't waste our two hours. Let's start another chapter. (*Looking at her notes*) The Visit to the Cairo Museum. The Fabulous Treasures of Tutankhamun.
(*Enter* ANA. *Arab music. She shrinks shyly into a corner, and starts to cry.* JUAN *pesters her by grimacing and making obscene gestures.*)

SANTIAGO: I devote the following morning to the enamel helmets, the necklaces of turquoise and lapis lazuli, the coral brooches, and the golden statuettes of King Tutankhamun.

KATHIE: Hidden among masks and hundreds of other beautiful objects, there was a poor helpless blonde girl weeping like a statue of Mary Magdalene.

SANTIAGO: All at once, 'midst the splendour of crystal urns, palanquins, sedan chairs, sumptuously adorned sarcophagi and shimmering caskets, I spy a ravishing young beauty with honeyed complexion and exquisite features, sobbing uncontrollably . . . What can have happened to her?

KATHIE: She was a German tourist. The stupid girl had gone out alone to sight-see in the streets of Cairo in a miniskirt. She'd caused such a commotion that she'd had to go inside the museum to escape the rabble.

SANTIAGO: Fleeing from the licentious looks, the importunate hands, the lascivious gestures, the illicit thoughts, and the extravagant displays of appreciation which her long pale legs provoked in the streets of Cairo, she had come to seek asylum amongst the wonders of Ancient Egypt. She reminded me of the girl Victor Hugo once described as obscene, because she was so innocent. Taking pity on her, I offered her my help.

ANA: (*Sarcastically*) It's you who should be pitied . . . Mark Griffin.

SANTIAGO: (*Without looking at her*) Go to hell.

(KATHIE *carries on dictating without seeing* ANA.)

ANA: I went some time ago, Mark Griffin. You sent me there, with a millstone round my neck. Have you forgotten already? Cast your mind back, Mark Griffin, try and remember.

(*As* SANTIAGO *and* ANA *talk,* KATHIE *carries on revising her notes and dictating as if* SANTIAGO *were still at his desk by the tape-recorder.*)

SANTIAGO: (*Getting to his feet*) I can't go on living in this house a moment longer. As far as I'm concerned, marriage is a totally meaningless institution. It's how you feel about other people that's important. I don't love you any more. I can't carry on living with a woman I don't love, my principles won't allow it. I suppose you're going to cry, make a scene, threaten me with suicide, do what most middle-class women do when their husbands leave them. Behave like a sensible, grown-up woman with a mind of her own, for a change.

ANA: All right. I won't make a scene. I won't force you to stay. But what should I tell the children?

SANTIAGO: So it's blackmail, is it? You're going to accuse me

of abandoning the children, is that it? Do you want me
to lose my respect for you into the bargain? Stop acting
like a woman who's seen too many soap operas on
television. Just because a marriage breaks up it doesn't
mean it's the end of the world for the children.

ANA: Oh, I dare say they'll survive. I'm asking you what I
should tell them, how I explain to them that their father
is not going to live with them any more. I'm not arguing
with you or blackmailing you. I'm asking your advice.
They're very young. They'll be very upset. Just tell me
what to say to them so they won't be so hurt.

SANTIAGO: Tell them the truth. Or do you think it's preferable
to lie to them – to indulge that hypocritical middle-class
habit just to spare their feelings a little longer?

ANA: So I tell them the truth, do I? I tell them their father has
run off because he's fallen in love with one of his pupils?

SANTIAGO: Exactly. It could've happened to you. It may even
happen to them, later. And if they're at all in touch with
their emotions, and don't grow up into repressed middle-
class women, they'll follow my example – like mature
rational beings.

(*He returns to his desk and sits, ready to carry on with the
recording.*)

ANA: Do you really think you're mature and rational, Mark
Griffin? Now that you're writing that travel book about
the journeys of Mrs Kathie Kennety through the Far East
and Black Africa – the book she supplies the ideas for
while paying you to put them into words – can you honestly
keep criticizing middle-class women with a clear
conscience, Mark Griffin?

(*She leaves him and moves towards* JUAN. *A few bars of Arab
music are heard.*)

KATHIE: Then I went to the old part of Cairo, and saw a little
church where the Virgin Mary had taken refuge with the
infant Jesus during the flight into Egypt. It was very
beautiful.

SANTIAGO: To my joy and delight, history and religion
intermingle in that kaleidoscopic maze of eternal alleyways

which constitutes the old quarter of Cairo. And this secluded chapel mellowed by time, which looms before me so gracefully and discreetly through clouds of dust – what could it be? Is it the sanctuary where Mary and the baby Jesus sheltered on their flight into Egypt?

KATHIE: And then I visited another little church, Jewish, I think, where Abraham was once supposed to have been.

SANTIAGO: (*Dictating*) Why do the walls of this timeless synagogue exude that other-worldliness which thrills me to the marrow? Because upon its stones the feet of the Patriarch Abraham once left their sacred imprint.

KATHIE: And finally I stopped at a shop which sold perfume.

SANTIAGO: And as in Egypt the material and the spiritual worlds are inseparable, I find myself almost immediately out in the dazzling morning sunlight on the threshhold of a perfumery.

KATHIE: It was late afternoon actually.

SANTIAGO: (*Correcting*) I find myself almost immediately in the crimson evening twilight on the threshhold of a perfumery.

KATHIE: There were some tourists there too. The perfume-seller explained in his disreputable English that the shop was very old, and he gave us some samples to try. He would keep on staring at me and in the end I became quite nervous.

SANTIAGO: The perfume-seller is tall and slim, with jet-black eyes and gleaming teeth. His gaze never leaves me, as he explains in French, the language of seduction, that the perfumery is as ancient as the earliest Egyptian mosques and that its craftsmen manufacture essences, the secret of which has been handed down from father to son throughout the centuries. He makes us sample exotic elixirs whose fragrance lasts for years on the skin. And as he talks, those lewd, hungry, lascivious eyes of his remain steadily fixed upon me.

(*As he has been talking,* SANTIAGO *has got up and has now taken on the guise of a passionate young man. He is very close to* KATHIE.)

KATHIE: Victor! What are you doing here? What do you want?

SANTIAGO: To run away with you, to elope with you. Yes,
Pussikins. It's all arranged. I've got hold of a van, I've
persuaded that little priest in Chincheros, and they've lent
me a house in the country.

KATHIE: Are you serious, Victor?

SANTIAGO: Don't you think it's a romantic idea? Wouldn't it
be romantic to run away and get married in secret to the
man you love despite your parents' wishes? Wouldn't it be
romantic to ditch that imbecile they're always trying to
foist on you? Aren't you always telling me what a romantic
girl you are?

KATHIE: You've got it all wrong. My parents have nothing to
do with my decision to marry Johnny. They're not forcing
me to marry him, nobody is. I'm marrying him because I
want to. Because . . . I love him.

SANTIAGO: That's not true. You're marrying Johnny because
your family have been ramming him down your throat
for the last I don't know how long so you'll forget about
me. You're not in love with that moron, don't try and
pretend you are.

KATHIE: You mustn't say things like that about Johnny. He's
my fiancé and he's going to be my husband.

SANTIAGO: (*Trying to kiss her*) But you're in love with me,
Pussikins. Haven't you told me so countless times? Do
you want me to remind you about all those things you used
to say to me in your letters? You're making a big mistake,
my love. Marry Johnny and you'll regret it for the rest of
your life.

KATHIE: I'll never regret it, I'm going to be very happy with
Johnny. So stop following me around, stop ringing me
up, and leave me alone. Just accept the fact once and for
all: I'm going to marry Johnny.

SANTIAGO: I'll never accept it. I won't give up till the very last
moment: not till you're walking down the aisle together.

KATHIE: Then you're going to be wasting your time miserably.

SANTIAGO: (*Returning to his place of work and his tape-recorder,
becoming himself again*) It's just that if I ever manage to
convince myself there's no more hope, that there's no . . .

99

KATHIE: (*To an invisible Victor*) What will you do? Will you kill me? Will you kill Johnny?

SANTIAGO: You know it doesn't sound very Egyptian, señora. Instead of Johnny, you need an Arab name. What about Ahmed? Or Gamul? Don't you like Gamul, the prurient perfume-seller, or Ahmed, the amorous parfumier.

KATHIE: Oh, Johnny's got nothing to do with my book. My mind was wandering. I was thinking of when I was young.

SANTIAGO: Stay young please, señora.

KATHIE: If you really meant that, you'd call me Kathie.

SANTIAGO: I'm sorry. From now on I'll call you Kathie, I promise.

KATHIE: I was thinking of my admirers. I had masses of them: Kike, Bepo, Harry, Gordo Rivarola . . . In those days, I was what was called a good match.

SANTIAGO: I know. I knew you, though you didn't know me. In fact everybody knew you. From the social columns, from society magazines.

KATHIE: What were you like in those days?

SANTIAGO: (*Dreamily*) Me? An idealist, a romantic. I dreamt I was going to be another Victor Hugo, I was going to dedicate my life to poetry, politics, art. Something important, where I could make my mark in society. I wanted to fill my life with grand gestures.

JUAN: (*Moving closer*) Can we talk for a moment, Kathie? It's about . . . Victor.

KATHIE: I've absolutely nothing to say about Victor. I don't want to talk about him. Either now or ever, with you or anyone else for that matter. I haven't seen him since we got married, so you needn't start making jealous scenes about him now.

(SANTIAGO *has left his place of work, and is now beside them. He seems overcome with grief.*)

SANTIAGO: So you married that clown after all, Pussikins. You're not the romantic girl you led me to believe you were in your letters.

JUAN: (*Uncomfortably*) I know you haven't seen him since we got married. And I'm not going to make any jealous scenes about him either. Have I ever done that? I trust you implicitly, my love. It's just that . . . he came to see me. (*Turning towards* SANTIAGO *in surprise*) You? But what a surprise, Victor! Come in, come in. Well, where did you spring from all of a sudden?

KATHIE: (*Aside; transfixed with fear*) Dear heavens! Victor! Victor! How could you have done such a thing! And all because of me, it was all my fault. You did do it because of me, didn't you?

SANTIAGO: (*Offering* JUAN *his hand*) How are you, Johnny? You seem surprised to see me. Yes, I suppose it's understandable. I don't want to take up your time, I imagine you're very busy. I just came to bring you these letters.

KATHIE: Yes, I'm sure it was because of me that you did it. I'll never forgive myself, I'll regret it for the rest of my life. How are you? Are you miserable? Are you happy? Have you at least found peace of mind?

JUAN: (*Leafing through the letters with increasing amazement*) What are these letters? Why, they're love letters. Letters from my wife to you. What does this mean, Victor? Why have you brought them here?

KATHIE: (*Grief-stricken*) Even if you're in the furthest corner of the earth, ensconced behind walls of solid stone, even if we never see each other again, I'll always be beside you, I'll always be with you, Victor.

SANTIAGO: As a sign of friendship, Johnny. Pussikins is your wife now. I'm sure neither you nor she would like those letters to get into the wrong hands. She wrote them to me when she was my girlfriend. When you read them you'll see that our relationship was always pure and innocent. I've brought you them, so you can tear them up or keep them, or do whatever you like with them.

KATHIE: (*Very tenderly*) With you I awaken at dead of night, the sky all aglow with myriad stars, having scarcely slept four hours on your mattress of straw, in that stark dank cell with its granite walls.

JUAN: (*Becoming more and more bewildered*) Ah, so that's the reason . . . Look, I don't quite know what to say to you. You've taken me rather by surprise. I . . . well, to tell you the truth, the fact is, I don't really know what to say.

KATHIE: I meditate kneeling on icy stone floors in front of that skull which stares down upon us as much as to say, 'I'm waiting for you.' With you I weep for the evil men do, that has turned the world into a poisonous cesspool.

SANTIAGO: Well, you might at least thank me.

KATHIE: I scourge myself, and wear a hair shirt, and I try and try till my strength ebbs away, to atone for that boundless talent man has for harming himself and his fellow men.

JUAN: For these letters? Yes, of course, thank you very much. (*Looking at him mistrustfully*) But this must be some sort of a trick, Victor? Surely you're pulling my leg?

KATHIE: With you I fast, in perpetual silence I live, barefoot I walk in the raw mid-winter and wear thick woollen garments in the searing summer heat. With you I till the soil with my own bare hands and with you I give succour and fodder to the rabbits.

SANTIAGO: No, Johnny, I'm not. I promise you.

KATHIE: With you I sing psalms to keep the world from splitting asunder and write eulogies to the wasp, the magnolia, the thistle, the fieldmouse, the laurel, the pollen and the ant.

JUAN: All right, I'm sorry. To tell you the truth, Victor, you've really rather thrown me. Well, I never! What a decent chap you are! Pussikins will be grateful to you as well. I'm sure she'd be quite upset if these letters were to go astray, now that she's a married woman.

KATHIE: For you I've renounced the world of the serpent, the tawdry pomp, the anguish and the ulcers, for a life of slavery which to me is freedom, of martyrdom which is happiness, of death which is life.

SANTIAGO: That's why I brought you them, I was thinking of her.

KATHIE: (*Anxious, tense*) And do you know why, Victor? Have you sensed it, have you guessed? Do you know?

JUAN: (*Confidentially*) You've taken a great weight off my mind,

Victor. I thought you felt bitter about me, I thought you hated me.

KATHIE: Because I love you. Yes, yes, yes, Victor. I love you! I love you! I've always loved you! Always, always, always.

SANTIAGO: Why? Because Pussikins married you? What a fantastic notion, Johnny. I felt a bit hurt to begin with but then I got used to the idea. Now I think it was the best thing all round that she should have married you.

KATHIE: (*Elated, ecstatic*) Yes, what you hear is true. Your Adèle loves you, she has always loved you, and she always will love you. My master, my mentor, my guru, my lord and king. Oh, Victor, Victor.

JUAN: Of course, of course, I always thought so too. You and Pussikins are two very different people, you'd never have got on.

KATHIE: (*Sad again*) With you, the very air I breathed has vanished, the light from my eyes, the voice from my throat, the fire from my blood.

SANTIAGO: (*Turning to an imaginary* KATHIE) You didn't marry me because you thought I was after your money.

KATHIE: (*Still addressing the same phantom*) I didn't marry you out of sheer stupidity.

JUAN: (*Still to* SANTIAGO) Whereas Kathie and I got on famously together.

KATHIE: Because I was a coward and an ignoramus, because I was blind and frivolous.

SANTIAGO: (*To the same imaginary* KATHIE) How disappointing, Pussikins. I thought you were more of an idealist, more of a dreamer, more intellectually honest, I never thought you were so calculating, I credited you with more openness. You're not like Adèle Foucher, Adèle!

KATHIE: (*Mad with despair*) Forgive me! Forgive me!

JUAN: Look, Victor, now that we've got things straight, we must see each other again sometime. You must come round to the house and have a meal with us one of these days.

KATHIE: Turn round, come back, there's still time. Listen to me, answer me! Oh, Victor, come back!

SANTIAGO: (*To* JUAN) That won't be possible, Johnny. I'm

going on a journey. A very long one. and I don't think
I'll be coming back to Peru again.

KATHIE: I want to be your servant, your slave, your pet bitch.

JUAN: (*To* SANTIAGO) That sounds very mysterious.

KATHIE: I want to be your whore, Victor.

SANTIAGO: You're right. It is, in a way. Look, I'll tell you. I'm
going to Spain. To Burgos. I'm going to join the
Trappists.

KATHIE: I'll go down to the docks and I'll take off my clothes
before the grimiest of sailors. I'll lick their tattoos, on my
knees, if you like. Any little whim, Victor, any fantasy at
all. However mad, just give the word. Whatever you
command.

JUAN: You're going to join the what?

KATHIE: You can spit on me, humiliate me, thrash me, lend
me to your friends. Just come back, come back.

SANTIAGO: Of course, you don't know what they are. The
Trappists. They're a religious order. Very old, very strict.
A closed order. Yes, in a nutshell, I'm going to become a
monk.

KATHIE: Come back even if it's only to kill me, Victor.

JUAN: (*Bursting out laughing*) Sure you wouldn't rather become
a bullfighter? I knew you'd try pulling my leg sooner or
later. There's no keeping up with you, Victor.

KATHIE: (*Desolate, resigned*) But I know you can't hear me, that
you never will hear me. I know your Adèle has lost for
ever her reason for living, for dying and coming back to
life again.

SANTIAGO: I'm not pulling your leg. I'm going to join the
Trappists. I've had a calling. But that's not all. I'm asking
you to help me. I'm destitute. The fare to Spain is
expensive. I'm asking my friends to help me collect what
I need for a third-class fare on the *Sea Queen*. Could you
give me a little hand, Johnny?

KATHIE: (*To* JUAN) Why are you telling me all this? Why should
any of it matter to me?

JUAN: I'm telling you because you're my wife. Who else am I
going to tell if I don't tell you? Do you think it could be

true, all that about the Trappists, or the Trappers, or the Traipsers, or whatever they call themselves?

SANTIAGO: (*To* KATHIE) What use would your money be to me? How many times have I explained it to you? I don't want to be rich, I want to be happy. Is your daddy happy? Is Johnny happy? Well, maybe Johnny is, but that's not because he's rich but because he's stupid. With me you would have been happy, you'd have had the most memorable wedding night of all time, Adèle.

JUAN: (*To* KATHIE) To start with I didn't believe him, of course. I thought he'd come to touch me for some money, or to tell me some story or other. But now, I don't know. You should have heard him . . . He spoke like a priest, all softly and gently. Said he'd had a calling. What do you want me to do with these letters, Pussikins?

SANTIAGO: (*To* KATHIE) So we won't be living in Chincheros any more, the little village with the purest air in the mountains. And we won't be sharing that free, simple life, that healthy, frugal, intimate existence. I'm not reproaching you for it, Pussikins. On the contrary, I'm grateful to you. You've been the instrument through which something greater than both you and me has manifested itself and made me see clearly what is expected of me. Thank you for leaving me, Pussikins! Thank you for marrying Juan! In the monastery I'll always pray for you both to be happy.

(*He returns to his place of work.*)

JUAN: (*To* KATHIE) Of course I haven't read them! (*Regrets having lied.*) All right, yes, I read them. What romantic letters, Kathie! You were very much in love with Victor, weren't you? And I never even suspected it. I never suspected you were so romantic either. The things you wrote, Pussikins!

(*He smiles and seems to forget about* KATHIE. *He crouches down, poised, giving the impression that at any moment he might start to surf.*)

KATHIE: (*Lost in thought*) Johnny darling, Johnny darling . . . What a clown you turned out to be!

SANTIAGO: (*Without looking at* KATHIE, *lost in his own thoughts*)
Well, with a name like Johnny darling, he doesn't exactly
sound like a very serious man.

KATHIE: (*Glancing at* SANTIAGO, *who remains absorbed in his
fantasy world*) It would be such a relief if I could talk to
you about my disastrous marriage, Mark Griffin.

SANTIAGO: Tell me about it, Kathie. That's what I'm here for
– in this little Parisian attic. It's part of my job. Well,
what were the problems? Did Johnny darling treat you
badly?

KATHIE: I didn't quite realize it then. I do now, though. I
felt . . . let down. One, two, maybe three years had gone
by since we'd got married and life had become very tedious.
Could this really be what marriage was like – this dull
routine? Was this what I'd got married for?

SANTIAGO: What did your husband do?

KATHIE: He used to go to the Waikiki.

SANTIAGO: That surfers' club, on Miraflores beach?

KATHIE: Every day, winter and summer. It was the main
occupation of his life.

JUAN: (*Youthful, athletic, carefree, looking towards the horizon*) I
like it, and why shouldn't I? I'm young, I want to enjoy
life.

KATHIE: (*Absorbed in her thoughts*) But, Johnny darling,
Hawaiian surfing isn't the only way of enjoying life. Don't
you get tired of being in the sea all day? You'll soon start
growing scales.

JUAN: (*Looking straight ahead*) I like it more every day. And I'll
keep on doing more of it. Till either I'm dead – or I'm
so old I can't ride waves any more.

(SANTIAGO *finally looks at* JUAN; *it is as if he were creating
him with his look.*)

SANTIAGO: Did he really devote his life to riding waves? Didn't
he feel ashamed?

(*As he surfs,* JUAN *keeps his balance by paddling with his
hands, and by leaning from side to side to steady himself as
the waves tug him along tossing him up and down.*)

JUAN: Ashamed? Quite the reverse. It makes me feel proud, I

like it, it makes me happy. Why should I be ashamed?
What's wrong with surfing? I've surfed all over the world
– in Miraflores, Hawaii, Australia, Indonesia, South
Africa. What's wrong with that? It's the most fantastic
thing there is! I enter the water slowly, smoothly, gliding
along, teasing the waves, outwitting the waves, then
suddenly I dive, I slice through them, I cut across them,
harnessing them, taming them, on, on I go, further and
further, pulled by the undertow right up to the rollers
after they've broken. I get on to my board, and like a
jockey on the starting line, I size them up, getting their
measure, calculating, guessing. Which of these little
crinkles will grow and grow and become the best wave to
ride? That one! That one there! I can hardly wait. It's
thrilling. My muscles tingle! My heart pounds! Pum,
pum, pum. There's not a second to lose, Johnny! I get into
position, I wait poised, now, I slap the water, and we're
away, it's got me, it tows me along, I caught it just at the
very moment before it broke, I jump, I stand on the
board, I stretch up, crouch, stretch up again, it's all in the
hips now, it's all balance, experience, stamina, a battle of
wits. No, little wave, you won't knock me over! I've ridden
waves which could topple a skyscraper, I've tunnelled
under waves as sheer as cataracts, like gaping caverns, like
soaring mountains, I've ridden waves which, had I lost
my balance, would have smashed me to pieces, torn me
limb from limb, pulverized me. I've ridden waves through
jagged coral reefs, in seas infested with marauding sharks.
I've nearly been drowned a hundred times, nearly been
deafened, paralysed, maimed. I've won championships on
four continents and if I haven't won any in Europe it's
because the waves in Europe are lousy for surfing. Why
should I be ashamed of myself?

KATHIE: (*Still immersed in her dreams*) What do you spend all
these hours thinking about, sitting there on your
surfboard, in the middle of the sea?

JUAN: (*Scanning the horizon, the seascape*) How large will the next wave be? Will I get on to it? Will I miss it? Will it knock me over? Will it carry me safely to the shore?

SANTIAGO: Do you ever think of anything other than waves?

JUAN: Sometimes, when it's a flat calm, I think about the last little woman I fancied. The one I met yesterday, or the day before, or even this morning. Will she be easy? Will she be difficult? Will we make love? Will it be the first or the second time of asking? Will I have to work on her, delicately, skilfully? Will it take a long time? When and where will it happen? What will it be like? (*Becoming ashamed, like a child interrupted doing something naughty*) Sometimes, I get so excited, I have to think of rhombuses, cubes, triangles and parallelograms to calm myself down.

KATHIE: Of course, you even used to make love to the surfboard. I'm not surprised. And when you're on the top of the wave, flapping your arms about like a ragdoll, what do you think about?

JUAN: Will they be watching me from the terrace of the Waikiki? Will the bathers see me from the swimming pool or the beach? And what about the motorists on the Embankment? Will they be looking? Will they be praising me? Will they be envious?

SANTIAGO: And what do you feel?

JUAN: I feel that I'm growing, that I'm handsome and virile, that I'm a real man. I feel like a god. What's wrong with that?

KATHIE: Does it make any difference to you if I'm the one who's watching you, if I'm the one who's admiring you?

JUAN: It did, before we got married, yes. It doesn't now, though. It's funny, but now you're my wife and it's your duty to admire me, I only seem to do it for those other women – beautiful women I've just got to know, or known for a bit, or haven't yet met.

SANTIAGO: (*Lost in thought*) Did it never enter your head it might be a crime to waste your time like this, when there are so many creative, productive things to be done in life?

JUAN: (*Fighting the waves*) Of course it never entered my head. Nothing quite so daft ever would. Do I do anyone any

harm with my surfing? And if I stop, is that going to solve
anyone's problem? Is going to the bank any more creative
and productive than a good day's surfing, or making love
to a woman?

KATHIE: (*Distressed by her memories*) Was this how my married
life was going to be? Watching Johnny darling riding
waves and being unfaithful to me?

SANTIAGO: (*Thoughtfully*) The real middle classes were even
more bourgeois than the pamphlets made them out to be;
we used to hate them on principle or on ideological
grounds. I didn't deceive you there, Anita.

(ANA *approaches* SANTIAGO, *who seems not to see her.* KATHIE
continues with her reminiscences.)

KATHIE: Going to bed late, getting up late. Are you going to
the bank today, Johnny?

JUAN: For a short while, yes, just to keep up appearances. But
what do you say to meeting at the Waikiki at around one,
OK?

KATHIE: Those damned waves, those damned surfboards, those
damned championships, and those damned trips to
Hawaii. It was all so excruciatingly boring, staying in hotels
with synthetic lawns and plastic palm trees. And having
to watch them all, indulge them, fête them, flatter them,
compliment them, and then there was the tittle-tattle,
whose wife's sleeping with whose husband, which couples
have come together, fallen out, made it up again and
finally fallen out for good. Getting ready for drinks, dinner,
Hawaiian parties, hen parties, always waiting for the big
surprise. Going to the hairdresser, wearing new outfits,
having one's nails manicured. Same thing tomorrow and
the day after. Is this what it's going to be like for the rest
of your life, Kathie?

SANTIAGO: (*In a brusque, aggressive and sarcastic tone of voice*)
Stuff and nonsense. I know very well what the real
problem is, and so do you, Kathie Kennety. But you're
ashamed to admit it.

KATHIE: (*Without seeing him or hearing him*) Things will be
different when you have children, Kathie. Looking after

them, bringing them up, watching them grow, that will give your marriage meaning. Stuff and nonsense! They didn't change a thing, they didn't fill the vacuum. Now, instead of going to the Waikiki alone, you go with Alexandra, and sometimes with Alexandra and little Johnny too. Now instead of getting bored alone, you get bored *en famille*. Is this what marriage is all about? Is this what motherhood is all about? Is this what you dreamt of, yearned for, throughout your schooldays? Just to go through life watching some poor imbecile prancing about between the waves on a piece of balsa wood?

SANTIAGO: Stuff and nonsense! Pure fiction! Shall I tell you the truth of the matter? Kathie Kennety was getting bored because her sublime surf-rider was ignoring her, leaving her alone every night, unattended and uninterfered with. That surfer wasn't exactly Victor Hugo, was he, Adèle? What with all those waves, he'd completely lost his sexual appetite.

ANA: (*To* SANTIAGO) Are you speaking from personal experience? When you ran off with that other woman, you hardly touched me for months. You didn't have any waves to ride, and yet you seemed to lose your sexual appetite too.

SANTIAGO: (*Discovering* ANA) No, I didn't. I just didn't fancy you any more, that's all. I used to make love every day with Adèle. In fact several times a day. Nine times, on one occasion, like Victor Hugo on his wedding night. Didn't I, Adèle?

KATHIE: (*Transformed into a young and bright little coquette*) No, professor, you didn't. But don't worry, I won't give away your little secret. You could never manage it more than twice a day, and with a long break in between. Ha ha ha . . .

SANTIAGO: (*To* ANA, *furiously*) And I'll tell you something else. The thought of night used to fill me with dread because it meant I'd have to share a bed with you. That was why I left you.

KATHIE: (*Becoming herself again, but still lost in her memories*)

Going to bed . . . that got boring too, like going to the
Waikiki and all those parties.

ANA: (*To* SANTIAGO) In other words you behaved just like the
sort of person you claimed to loathe so vehemently: like
a good middle-class man. Didn't you use to say that it was
the most despicable thing in the world? Have you already
forgotten what you used to teach me? All those lectures
you gave me to make a free, liberated, emancipated
woman of me.

(SANTIAGO *declaims very seriously, to* ANA, *who listens to him
fascinated.* KATHIE, *who has now become Adèle, puts on
nail varnish and looks at him mockingly from time to time.*)

SANTIAGO: It's not passionate love, but love based on mutual
understanding. That's what our relationship will be,
Anita. Passionate love is a sham, a bourgeois swindle, a
fraud, an illusion, a trap. A relationship founded solely
on sexual attraction, in which everything is justified in the
name of pleasure, spontaneity and natural impulse, is bound
to be false and ephemeral. Sexual desire isn't everything
nor should it ever be, it isn't even what fundamentally
binds us together. No partnership can possibly last if it's
reliant solely on lust.

(KATHIE, *still Adèle, bursts out laughing, but* ANA *nods, trying
to understand.*)

KATHIE: (*Smiles; returning to being herself*) And yet, it was nice
to begin with, when we used to hug each other every
night and you used to say those naughty things to me,
Johnny darling. I used to go quite puce with
embarrassment, it made me dizzy, it was lovely. It seemed
everything was going to be as I'd always dreamt, that I'd
find meaning to life, that I'd be happy and fulfilled.

SANTIAGO: In a relationship based on mutual understanding,
sex is just one component amongst many and it isn't even
the most important, either. Such a relationship is founded
on a sharing of ideals, a spirit of selflessness, a struggle
for common causes, mutual participation in work, and a
feeling of moral, spiritual and intellectual empathy.

ANA: (*To* SANTIAGO) I tried to please you. I did everything you

asked me to do so that this special relationship you
described could flourish. Well, did I or didn't I? Didn't I
give up my job in the boutique? Didn't I take up
sociology, as you suggested, instead of interior design
which was what I really wanted to do?

JUAN: (*From his surfboard*) Am I or am I not as good in bed as
I am on the surfboard, Kathie? Am I or am I not better
than Victor Hugo, Adèle?

KATHIE: You are, Johnny darling. That's why so many young
girls are always throwing themselves into your arms.
Blondes, brunettes, redheads, yellowheads. That's why
you're unfaithful to me in so many different languages
and on so many different continents, Johnny darling.

ANA: (*To* SANTIAGO) Didn't I try to please you by wearing what
you wanted me to wear? I stopped putting on lipstick,
nail varnish, and make-up, because you said it was frivolous
and bourgeois. And what did I gain by trying to please
you? I stopped pleasing you, that's what.

SANTIAGO: (*To* KATHIE, *all sweetness and flattery*) You know,
you've got very pretty hair, Adèle.

(KATHIE *is transformed into Adèle; she seems to coo and croon.*)

KATHIE: So that it stays that way – soft, shiny, wavy and
bouncy, I give it one of my special treatments twice a
week. Shall I tell you what it is, professor? But you mustn't
breathe a word about it to the other girls in the faculty.
Promise? You take one egg yolk, an avocado pear and three
teaspoonfuls of oil. You put them all in the liquidizer for
half a minute, then you daub the paste all over your hair
and leave it to dry for three-quarters of an hour. You then
wash it with a good shampoo and rinse it. It looks nice,
don't you think?

SANTIAGO: (*Entranced*) Very nice indeed: soft, shiny, bouncy
and wavy. You've get pretty hands too, Adèle.

KATHIE: (*Looking at them, showing them off*) To stop them from
getting rough and the skin from getting hard, and so that
they look smooth and silky like two little Persian kittens,
I've got a little secret for them too. Or rather, I've got
two little secrets. Every morning for ten minutes I give

them a good rub with lemon juice and, every night, for
another ten minutes with coconut milk. They look nice,
don't they?

SANTIAGO: (*Entranced*) Yes, as smooth and silky as two little
Persian kittens. Whenever I catch a glimpse of them in
the lectures, they remind me of two tiny white doves,
fluttering across the desks.

KATHIE: Ah, what a poetic little compliment! Do you really
like them that much, professor?

SANTIAGO: I like everything about you, your hair, your nose,
your eyes . . . Why do you call me 'professor'? Why are
you always making fun of me?

KATHIE: Well, aren't you my professor? It's a question of
respect. What would my fellow students say if they heard
me call the first-year lecturer in Golden Age Literature,
Mark – Mark Griffin?

SANTIAGO: Is that why you address me so formally?

KATHIE: You should always address older people formally.

SANTIAGO: In other words you think I'm ancient.

KATHIE: Not ancient, no. Just an older man. Who's married,
with two little daughters. Do you have a photo of them
in your wallet that you can show me?

SANTIAGO: You know you're very wicked, Adèle?

KATHIE: A lot of people like me for it.

SANTIAGO: Yes. I do, for one. I like you very much. You know
that, don't you?

KATHIE: It's the first I'd heard of it. And what is it you like
most about me?

SANTIAGO: You're such a flirt.

KATHIE: Do you really think I'm a flirt?

SANTIAGO: The very devil in person.

KATHIE: Now tell me what you don't like about me.

SANTIAGO: The fact that you refuse to go out with me.

KATHIE: You crafty old thing, professor.

SANTIAGO: Seriously though, Adèle, why won't you? Bourgeois
prejudice? What's wrong with going to the cinema
together, for instance? Or listening to a little music?

KATHIE: All right, I accept. But on one condition.

SANTIAGO: Whatever you want.

KATHIE: That we take your wife and two little girls with us. And now, I'm going off to study. I don't want you giving me bad marks. If you behave yourself, I'll let you into another secret some time: I'll tell you how I keep my teeth sparkling and my eyes shining, how I stop my nails from breaking, and why I never get freckles or a double chin. *Ciao*, professor.

SANTIAGO: *Ciao*, Adèle. (*To himself*) She's so gorgeous, so delicious, so exciting.

ANA: And I stopped being gorgeous, delicious and exciting because you said it was frivolous and bourgeois.

SANTIAGO: (*Pensively*) Well, it was. (*Discovering* ANA) It is, Anita. Am I to blame if it's the frivolous, bourgeois women that happen to turn me on? Is it my fault if all these free liberated women are so earnest and sober that they leave me absolutely cold, Anita? A leopard can't change his spots. Moral principle and political persuasion carry no weight at all when it's a matter of basic human nature.

ANA: But how come? Didn't you teach me there was no such thing as human nature?

SANTIAGO: (*Pontificating*) It doesn't exist. Human nature doesn't exist, Anita. It's just another piece of bourgeois trickery to justify the exploitation of the masses, Anita.

ANA: You miserable cheat! You liar!

SANTIAGO: (*Magisterial*) Man is made of malleable stuff, Anita. Everyone makes of himself what he chooses, Anita! Only thus can one have faith in the progress of humanity, Anita! You really must read Jean-Paul Sartre, Anita!

ANA: You really led me up the garden path, Mark Griffin.

SANTIAGO: (*Pensive again*) Jean-Paul Sartre really led me up the garden path, Anita.

KATHIE: (*Becoming herself again*) That's something you could never do, Johnny darling. I always saw through you straight away.

JUAN: (*Still concentrating on the waves*) That time you caught

me with Maritza, you scratched my face so savagely the
mark lasted for two whole weeks.

KATHIE: Every time you were unfaithful to me, I felt as if I'd
been branded with a red-hot iron. Lying awake at night,
weeping, I thought the world was coming to an end, I used
to grind my teeth with the humiliation of it all. I began
to lose weight; I started to get bags under my eyes; I made
scenes.

JUAN: How they laughed at me at the Waikiki when they saw
those scratches!

ANA: If, instead of trying to live up to your anti-bourgeois
principles, I'd paid more attention to my mother, you
might never have gone off with Adèle.

SANTIAGO: (*Pensively*) And what advice did that petit-bourgeois
social climber from Santa Beatriz give you? Always
hobnobbing with the smart set in Orrantia.

KATHIE: (*Lecturing* ANA, *as if she were her small daughter*) You've
got to be quite ruthless with men, Anita. You've got to use
a bit of cunning. Your husband may be an intellectual or
what have you, but what really counts in life is sex. Now
I may not know the first thing about intellectuals, but I
know quite a lot about sex. If you don't want to lose him,
if you don't want him to go out with too many other
women, keep him in suspense, and don't ever let him
take you for granted.

ANA: And what do I do to keep Santiago in suspense, Mummy?

KATHIE: Keep him on a tight rein then give him his head from
time to time. You play the perfect lady by day and the
degenerate whore by night. Perfume, music, mirrors, every
kind of luxury, the more bizarre and decadent the better:
let him drown with joy! But not every day: only when you
decide and when it suits you. Keep him on a tight rein.
From time to time the whore can turn frigid; for a week
or so, the courtesan may wear a veil. And, as a last resort,
there's always jealousy. The sudden exit, the mysterious
phone call, ostentatious little whispers to friends at
parties, contrariness, sighing. Let him suspect all he likes,
let him be consumed with jealousy! It may cost you a

knock or two but so what? There's no such thing as love without the odd blow! Keep him in suspense and you'll have him all over you morning, noon and night!

ANA: You trusted me blindly and that's what finished it. But that Adèle, she really put you through the hoop, and you ran after her like a dog, Mark Griffin.

JUAN: Jealousy is fantastic, Pussikins! I only say that for the closeness one feels after it. You know, for all you say, you're very attractive when you're jealous. The best love-making we've ever had has been after a row. Like in Hawaii, when you caught me with that Eurasian girl on the beach. You were so vicious to her, Kathie. But how exquisite it was afterwards, how exquisite! We made love on the sand, and then in the sea, then on that artificial lawn, remember, and then in the sea again. Wasn't it fabulous, darling?

KATHIE: Not that fabulous really, no.

JUAN: Well, if you really want to know, Kathie, you're not that good at it, you're not exactly what one might call a sexual athlete. In fact you're quite . . . uninteresting really. You yawn, you fall asleep, you get embarrassed, you burst out laughing. The trouble is, darling, you don't take sex seriously! And it's the most serious thing in the world! It's like surfing, Kathie!

KATHIE: Some people have happier recollections of my talents, Johnny darling.

(JUAN and ANA disappear.)

SANTIAGO: (In a slightly aggressive, sarcastic tone of voice) The prurient perfume-seller of Cairo, for instance?

KATHIE: What exactly are you trying to say, Mr Mark Griffin?

SANTIAGO: You know very well, you poor menopausal little rich girl, you neurotic millionairess, you pseud, you exploiter of progressive intellectuals. You know very well, Kathie Kennety.

KATHIE: (Without being the slightest bit perturbed) What do I know very well?

SANTIAGO: (With ferocious aggressiveness, as if baring some old wounds and feelings of festering resentment) You don't go

travelling to all these exotic places just to satisfy your
aesthetic curiosity and your spiritual hankerings, but so
that you can trull around without fear of what people might
say. You can go on luxury holidays, full of memorable
experiences, exotic perfumes and seductive music; you can
indulge in outlandish, elaborate love affairs, at a safe
distance from your society friends in Lima. Black men,
yellow men, Arabs, Eskimos, Afghans, Hindus! Every
cock in the world at your disposal! I wonder, did they
charge, like I do, by the hour? How much did the
amorous perfume-seller from Cairo charge for putting on
his little act, for pretending to lust after you, you depraved
woman?

KATHIE: (*Who has been listening to him amiably, faintly amused*)
Aren't you overstepping the mark, Mr Griffin? Aren't you
infringing the basic laws of common courtesy between an
employee and his boss? You're asking me questions I
can't possibly answer without seeming ill-bred or improper.
(SANTIAGO's *anger starts to abate. He sounds demoralized.*)

SANTIAGO: No, I haven't forgotten you're the boss, you cheap
writer of trash, you would-be literata; you can't even spell
properly. I hate you. If you didn't pay me, I'd merely
despise you, I might possibly pity you. Because it must
be tedious, mustn't it, to take trips round the world over
land and sea, travelling about from continent to continent,
squandering a fortune in the process, and writing books
which you don't actually write at all, and which nobody
reads anyway, just so that you can indulge in a bit of casual
love-play from time to time. It must be extremely tedious,
isn't it, Kathie Kennety?
(*He has positioned himself behind his tape-recorder again and
started to dictate, moving his lips in silence.* KATHIE *looks at
him now with wistful admiration. The Parisian music heard
at the beginning of the play starts to be heard again in the
distance.*)

KATHIE: The tedious thing about it is having to shut myself up
day and night in this little attic, and deprive myself of all
the marvellous things Paris has to offer, which are just

there on my doorstep. All I have to do is go through that door and down the hotel staircase. Whereas you, Mark Griffin, you must really appreciate the bright lights of the city when you leave this room. If I didn't have to work on this book on Black Africa and the Far East, would you let me go with you? I wouldn't say a word, I'd be no trouble at all. I'd learn so much, going to art galleries, libraries, theatres, concerts, lectures and bistros with you. Of course I'd feel ignorant and small, listening to you converse with all those brilliant friends of yours who've read every book and know everything about everything. (SANTIAGO *carries on dictating, as is clear from the movement of his lips, but he is obviously enjoying listening to her.*) Because that's your life, Mark Griffin, apart from the two short hours you spend here, isn't that so? Sauntering along the banks of the Seine, browsing in second-hand bookstalls, going to every concert, ballet and opera, attending symposia at the Collège de France, keeping up with the latest foreign films and never missing a private view. How wonderful it must be to sit up all night discussing philosophy with Jean-Paul Sartre, feminism with Simone de Beauvoir, anthropology with Lévi-Strauss, theatre with Jean-Louis Barrault, and fashion with Pierre Cardin! I'd listen to them, fascinated, awestruck at such intellectual wizardry. How marvellous your life must be, Mark! How rich and full! Whereas mine, incarcerated here in this attic, seems so petty and insignificant by comparison. But our two hours are nearly up. Let's carry on. Let's return to Cairo, to the ancient city, to that little street with the perfume shop . . .
(*Far off, the Arab music comes to life again.*)

SANTIAGO: (*Dictating*) . . . Shortly I'm to discover what it is the wily perfume-seller is suggesting. With cloying charm, he begs me to wait, while he attends to the other tourists. He brings me a cup of tea and, I, naïve as I am, accept and remain in the shop.

KATHIE: Don't you think that bit about 'naïve as I am' sounds a trifle vulgar?

SANTIAGO: Yes. Yes, it does. And I, stupid as I am, remain in
the shop . . .

KATHIE: Doesn't it sound a bit unsubtle – 'stupid as I am'?

SANTIAGO: (*Correcting*) Yes. And I, er, I remain in the
shop . . .

KATHIE: Then before you could say knife, the craftsmen
disappeared and the perfume-seller started to take out
some jars; he put them in front of me and offered me them.
Then he suddenly began to take out some trinkets and
jewels as well.

(SANTIAGO *has got to his feet and is doing what, according to*
KATHIE, *the Cairo perfume-seller did. Arab music with
hornpipes, flutes, bongo drums, castanets, seems to waft through
the air.*)

SANTIAGO: Make your choice, my foreign beauty, make your
choice! Here I have lotions, pure essence of perfume, life-
giving elixirs, balsam and lacquers. To put on your hair,
behind your ears, on your neck, your breasts, under your
arms, on your navel, your groin, between your toes and on
the soles of your feet! Choose, oh choose, my foreign
beauty! For here I have necklaces, ear-rings, watches,
powder-cases, bracelets, bangles, anklets, diadems! Made
out of amber, tortoiseshell, lapis lazuli, butterfly wings!

KATHIE: (*Pleased yet intimidated*) Thank you very much,
monsieur. Your perfumes are ravishing, and your jewels
are quite dazzling. But I don't wish to buy anything. Thank
you very much all the same, monsieur, you've been most
helpful and kind.

(SANTIAGO *ingratiating, snakelike, circles hypnotically round*
KATHIE *moving his hands and rolling his eyes.*)

SANTIAGO: But who's talking of buying anything, my foreign
beauty, who's thinking about filthy money, oh my
beautiful exotic foreigner from the exotic kingdom of Peru?
Everything I have is yours. Everything in this shop is
yours. Choose whatever you want, take it away with you.
Take it as a tribute to your beauty!

KATHIE: Your generosity overwhelms me and confuses me,
monsieur. But I can't accept presents from strangers. I'm

a respectable woman, a Catholic, I come from Lima, and I have a family. I'm not one of those light-minded tourists you're no doubt accustomed to, monsieur.

SANTIAGO: I'm an amorous perfume-seller, madame. Let me take you for a stroll through Cairo by night, let me introduce you to those secret little pleasure dens, those sacred temples of sensual delight. Cairo is the most corrupt city in the world, madame!

KATHIE: Control yourself, monsieur. Behave like a gentleman, like a respectable human being. Don't come so close. Take your filthy hands off me!

SANTIAGO: We'll go to see the pyramids, bathed by the moonlight and barefoot we'll walk in the cool of the desert. We'll visit a night-club where houris do the belly dance, their boneless bodies writhing in ecstasy. Dawn will discover us peacefully sleeping, lulled by the charm of those aphrodisiac melodies which make serpents hiss and give camels orgasms.

KATHIE: Help! Help! Don't touch me! You filthy Indian! You miserable mulatto! You disgusting halfbreed! Let go of me or I'll kill you! Ah, you didn't know, did you, that Kathie Kennety is ready and able to challenge villains the whole world over? Hands up or I'll shoot!

(*She threatens him with a small woman's pistol and* SANTIAGO *returns to his place of work. He continues dictating. An alarm clock start to ring.*)

SANTIAGO: When he sees the little revolver the perfume-seller releases me. Rapidly I leave the perfume shop and lose myself in the dusty narrow alleyways of the old city . . .

KATHIE: While I was going back to the hotel, I shuddered at the thought of that fat, coarse, impertinent . . .

SANTIAGO: And as I wind back and forth, asking my way, through that labyrinth of streets which is old Cairo, I eventually find the road back to the hotel, and my whole body squirms in sheer revulsion as I recall the alchemist's embrace, and my nostrils still detect the pungent aroma of his perfumes, as if they were poison . . .

(*The alarm finishes.*)

KATHIE: Ah, how quickly the two hours went today . . .
SANTIAGO: They flew past. But we did some good work, didn't
we, Kathie?
(*They smile at each other.*)

ACT TWO

The set is the same. As the house lights go down, we hear the Parisian music which sets the atmosphere for Kathie Kennety's little attic: it could be 'Les feuilles mortes', 'J'attendrai toujours' or something equally well known and dated. The four characters are on stage, but the lighting is focused on SANTIAGO *— who is sitting in his usual place of work, dictating into the tape-recorder — and* KATHIE, *who strolls around the room with a bundle of papers and maps in her hands, recalling memories and relating incidents from the past. The Parisian melody is replaced by some African music: tribal drums throb, wild beasts grunt, and birds sing, against the thunderous roar of a waterfall. In an imaginary parody of the scene,* ANA *and* JUAN *may mime what is being narrated.*

KATHIE: The first night at the Murchison Falls, I was woken up by a frightful noise.

SANTIAGO: It is a windswept moonlit night on the shores of Lake Victoria, on the edge of the Murchison Falls. All of a sudden mysterious noises tear into the velvety darkness of the African night, and I wake up.

KATHIE: It wasn't the waterfalls but some other noise. The hotel was full, and so they'd put me in a tent in the garden. The canvas was flapping about in the wind and looked as though it would take off at any moment.

SANTIAGO: The flimsy bedouin tents of the encampment where they'd given me shelter quiver as if made of rice paper.

KATHIE: I threw on my clothes, and I went out to see what all the fuss was about.

SANTIAGO: Frightened and bewildered, I sit bolt upright in my hammock; I grope for the mosquito net which I draw aside as I reach for my revolver with the mother-of-pearl handle which I keep under my pillow.

KATHIE: What was happening? What was going on?

SANTIAGO: What is happening? What is going on? Are the waterfalls overflowing? Is the lake flooding its banks? Is it an earthquake? Is our camp being attacked by a herd of elephants? Or a tribe of cannibals?

KATHIE: Nothing like that. Two hippos were fighting over a 'hippa'.

SANTIAGO: (*Switching off his tape-recorder for an instant*) Hippopotamuses? Was that what woke you up? Two hippopotamuses fighting over a hippopotama?

KATHIE: Shouldn't you say female hippopotamus?

SANTIAGO: You should say whatever sounds best. Hippopotama has more of a ring to it, it's more incisive, more original. (*Dictating again*) Is the lake overflowing? Is it an earthquake? Is our camp being attacked by a herd of elephants? Or a tribe of cannibals? No. Once again it's that old eternal love triangle, that familiar tale of lust, rape and revenge. In the murky mud on the banks of the Murchison Falls, roaring and thundering, two hippopotamuses fight to the death over a hippopotama . . .

KATHIE: It was pitch dark. You couldn't see a thing. But I realized by the noises they were making that it was a ferocious struggle.

SANTIAGO: (*More and more enthusiastically*) Prehistoric, massive and lumbering with their enormous heads, their huge bulbous bodies and their ridiculously small feet, I can just make them out through the thick dark shadows, fiercely biting each other on the flank.

KATHIE: The female waited skittishly, all of a twitter, as she coyly watched to see which of the males was going to win her.

SANTIAGO: Meanwhile, the coveted prize – she, who had provoked such pachidermal hatred and lust – the hippopotama – moves about, swinging her hips, aroused by the spectacle, as she waits eagerly to see who will win the combat. Will the victor have the right to . . . possess her? Attack her? Penetrate her?

KATHIE: Attack her is best. A German, or a Dutchman or someone, who was staying at Murchison Falls, an academic or a scientist, something like that, said the hippopotamus was a very strange animal.

SANTIAGO: (*In a strong German accent*) This primitive rough-skinned wrinkly creature which you see before you, Frau

Katharina, the hippopotamus, has such a delicate throat that it can only swallow little birds, flies, bumblebees and flutterbies who, mistaking it for a tree trunk, settle on it. But it's an animal with an unquenchable sexual appetite, a lustful beast with a seismic potency. It's not unusual after her first encounter for a hippopotama to be completely put off the idea of sex, rather like Adèle Foucher for instance, since even the most effete of hippopotami easily outdo the record established for the human species by Victor Hugo whose nine performances on his wedding night . . . (*Resuming his normal voice, carrying on dictating*) The Prussian zoologist was quite right: for the whole of the rest of the night we heard the hoofed victor and the contented hippopotama copulating with such a deafening report that it drowned the noise of the cataracts.

KATHIE: (*Laughing*) That bit about 'copulating with such a deafening report', I wonder what my children will say to that?

(ANA *and* JUAN, *who have now become* KATHIE's *children, rush towards her.*)

JUAN: What exactly are you writing, Mama? A travel book about Black Africa and the Far East, or a pornographic novel?

ANA: Do you want everyone to laugh at us?

(SANTIAGO *stops dictating.*)

SANTIAGO: Have your children got many hang-ups?

KATHIE: Yes, I suppose they have. At any rate they appear to in front of me. I wonder what they're like when they're alone. Or with their friends, or with their lovers? I wonder if my children have lovers.

JUAN: We've got a surprise for you, Mama, which you're going to love.

SANTIAGO: You don't talk much about your family, you know.

ANA: Can't you guess what it is, Mama? The tickets! For your tour of Black Africa and the Far East!

KATHIE: This is a travel book, not an autobiography, that's why I don't mention them.

JUAN: Forty-two countries, and over eighty cities.

ANA: Every race, religion, language and landscape under the sun. You'll hardly have time to turn round, Mama.

SANTIAGO: Did it take a lot to persuade them to let you go on such a long trip?

KATHIE: It didn't take anything at all, quite the reverse in fact. (*Turns towards her children.*) Of course I'll have time to turn round. Why were you in such a hurry to buy the tickets? I haven't even decided if I'm going yet.

JUAN: Because you're dying to go – you just needed a little push. So we gave you one.

ANA: You're going to learn so much, Mama. All those different countries, all those exciting foreign places. All that experience and think of all the adventures you'll have. You'll be able to use them in your book.

JUAN: Of course, you'll be travelling first class and staying in five-star hotels, and you'll have a private car and personal guide on every excursion.

ANA: You deserve it, Mama!

KATHIE: (*Mocking*) Aren't you going to miss me?

JUAN: Of course we are. We're doing all this for you, so you can enjoy yourself, so you can write that book you've had on your mind for so long.

ANA: Aren't you always telling us how fed up you are with life in Lima, with its constant round of tea parties, luncheon parties, and weddings all over the place? That you never have any time for the really serious things in life what with all the social razzmatazz? Well, there you are then, for eight months of the year you can concentrate entirely on getting a bit of culture.

JUAN: You'll be travelling on a diplomatic passport, so you won't have any difficulties with the customs.

KATHIE: What wonderful children I've got; you're both so good and kind. (*Changing her tone of voice*) You're just a couple of cynics, aren't you? You're glad to be getting rid of me.

JUAN: But how can you talk such utter nonsense, Mama? It's pointless even trying to make you happy. You're impossible. And we thought you'd be so thrilled with these tickets, we wanted to give you the time of your life.

ANA: You twist everything round so. Why should we want to get rid of you?

KATHIE: (*Rubbing her thumb and forefinger together*) Money, my little love, money. Who's going to be in charge of my affairs while I'm away? I'd have to give you *carte blanche* so you could do anything you wanted. Now wouldn't I?

JUAN: Of course you wouldn't. Honestly, you've got such a suspicious mind! I suppose this had to come up sooner or later.

KATHIE: Because you're brassed off with me poking my nose into everything, questioning everything. Do you think I don't know how it irritates you to have to get my permission for the least little thing?

ANA: It was unfortunate Johnny came up with that suggestion about the power of attorney . . .

KATHIE: Which would entitle you to share out everything I possess before I'm even dead.

JUAN: No, no, no. It was to save you any unnecessary worries, Mama, to save you spending your time in lawyers' offices, with boards of directors, in banks, and so on.

ANA: You're so paranoid, it's beyond belief, Mama!

KATHIE: I may be paranoid, but I'm not signing that power of attorney – I'm not dead just yet and I don't want to feel as if I am. You haven't managed to get your own way, so now you're sending me off round the world instead . . .

ANA: That's not fair, Mama!

JUAN: You were the one who wanted to go on this trip, we'd never even have thought of it.

ANA: (*To* JUAN) She's so ungrateful, it's incredible. Take back the tickets, Juancito. I wouldn't go to any more trouble on her account, if I were you.

KATHIE: The only trouble you went to was buying them, dear, and in case you've forgotten, I was the one who paid for them in the first place.

JUAN: All right, all right. Don't let's quarrel about it. We'll take back the tickets and there's an end to it.

KATHIE: No, don't. I've decided to go, and I'm going to write my book after all. But don't get too excited, I'm not going to get myself eaten by a tiger or squashed by an elephant, I'll be coming back all in one piece, to find out exactly what you've been up to with my money – my money, don't forget – while I've been away.

(JUAN *approaches* KATHIE. *He seems to want to strike up a silent conversation with her, but she declines, retreating into her private reverie.* ANA *approaches* SANTIAGO.)

ANA: You know, you're rather like a hippopotamus yourself, Mark Griffin. Don't try and pretend you're not listening. Well, wouldn't you agree you're like a hippopotamus?

SANTIAGO: How am I like a hippopotamus?

ANA: You look so strong and reliable, anyone would think you could take on a man-eating tiger. But it's all façade! When it comes down to it, all you can do is catch flies, beetles, butterflies and little birds.

SANTIAGO: (*Fantasizing*) I know how I'm like a hippopotamus . . .

KATHIE: (*Playing the role of Adèle*) My dear sweet professor, my love, pay no attention to that spiteful bitch. She's always trying to manipulate you, ignore her, don't let her sour our relationship.

SANTIAGO: (*Eagerly*) Of course I won't, my little Persian kitten! Now come here, let me smell your fragrance, let me tickle you and lick you. You're not going to get away from me this time.

KATHIE: (*Charmed by him, but also fearful*) You frighten me, Mark. You will start playing these games, but we both know where they're going to end up, don't we?

SANTIAGO: (*Lifting her up and parading her in his arms*) Must end up. But what does it matter? Aren't you pleased you can arouse such ardent passion in your husband, Adèle?

KATHIE: In my lover, you mean. I'm not your wife, it's that spiteful bitch.

SANTIAGO: No, she isn't. Not any more. Not since I left her for you, silly. Now you're my wife – as well as my pupil, my lover and my kitten.

KATHIE: Don't get so excited, my love. This is hardly the time. Didn't you have a lecture to give on the Spanish mystics?

SANTIAGO: The Spanish mystics can go to hell. Today I've got a lecture specially for you. And I'm going to give it to you now, over there, in the bedroom. Come, come.

KATHIE: (*Mesmerized*) What again, my angel? Have you gone quite mad? We made love last night and this morning.

SANTIAGO: (*Driven crazy*) And we'll do it again – before lunch, after lunch, at teatime and suppertime. We'll do it nine times a day. Did you hear that? Nine times!

KATHIE: Who'd have thought Professor Griffin capable of such feats?

SANTIAGO: It's all your fault, you awaken in me feelings of such passionate intensity, I'm like a vulcano about to erupt. When I see your little body, when I touch it and stroke it, when I hear your voice, when I smell your fragrance, my blood starts to course through my veins like a raging torrent.

KATHIE: (*Pouting*) But I'm not the only one who unleashes such storms, Victor. Do you think I don't know what you get up to with Juliette Drouet? And all those other ephemeral little flies that swarm around you? Do you think I don't know how many of them you've made love to?

SANTIAGO: (*Proud, seductive*) But these are minor escapades, Adèle. They don't impinge on either my feelings or my poetry. They're quite unimportant. No, the only use these little creatures have is to prove to me how incomparable you are, my Adèle *chérie*.

KATHIE: (*Sobbing*) When I think about you making love to them, I get so jealous. You've no idea how much I suffer.

SANTIAGO: Jealousy adds a certain piquancy to love. It makes it more exciting, it colours it, it gives it flavour.

KATHIE: But you go after anything in a skirt! Look at my nails. They used to be long and beautiful and now, just look at them! It's all your fault, it's all because of your treachery. Every time you go out, I get quite sick with anguish: which of those little insects will he be with this time? What'll he be saying to them? What'll he be doing to them? Where? And how many times? Nine?

SANTIAGO: Whether it's God, Mother Nature or the Devil, I

don't know. But talents have been bestowed upon me,
which set me apart from ordinary men. The gift of poetry
which in my case comes inextricably linked with an
infinite propensity for passionate love.

KATHIE: But don't we make love every day, Victor?

SANTIAGO: It's not enough, Adèle. I must satisfy these longings,
quench these flames.

KATHIE: You're one of nature's marvels!

SANTIAGO: I am.

KATHIE: You're insatiable, indefatigable, a colossus amongst
men.

SANTIAGO: I am.

KATHIE: You're Victor Hugo, Mark Griffin.

SANTIAGO: Just as other men need air, so I need women. I need
a constant supply or else I suffocate . . . Like the drinker
of absinthe, like the opium eater, I'm quite addicted to
them.

KATHIE: Your knowledge exceeds that of the *Kama Sutra*, the
Ananga Ranga, Giacomo Casanova, and the Marquis de
Sade.

SANTIAGO: It does. What do women feel when they make love
with me, Adèle *chérie*?

KATHIE: Like tropical butterflies pierced by a pin, like flies
struggling in a glutinous web, like chickens on a spit.
(ANA *who has been watching them sardonically, bursts out
laughing and breaks the spell. Attention is focused on* KATHIE
and JUAN.)

JUAN: (*Transformed back into Johnny darling*) And what about
our son?

KATHIE: (*Herself again*) My son! Poor boy! He didn't turn out
to be at all like his father. (*To* JUAN) You were just an
amusing rogue, a lovable playboy, Johnny darling. Your
only interest in money is spending it. Little Johnny, on
the other hand, is the most hard-working man in the world,
the most dependable, the most boring and the most
disagreeable. His only interest in money is making more
of it.

JUAN: That's not true, Kathie. You're maligning little Johnny.

KATHIE: I'm not maligning him. He's only interested in banking, boards of directors, rates of exchange, the price of shares and the property market. His sole concern in life is whether or not we'll ever have agrarian reform in this country.

SANTIAGO: (*Thinking aloud*) And do you know, Kathie, what agrarian reform would mean?

KATHIE: Taking away decent, respectable people's land and giving to the Indians. Sometimes I wish we would have agrarian reform if only to see the look on little Johnny's face.

JUAN: Have you got such a low opinion of your daughter too?

KATHIE: She's superficial and brainless. She takes after you there, Johnny darling. The new improved version. She doesn't think about anything except beaches, parties, clothes and men. In that order.

JUAN: I think you detest your children almost as much as you used to detest me, Kathie Kennety.

KATHIE: No. Not quite that much. Besides, they're the ones that hate me. Because I won't let them do what they want with my property.

JUAN: You'd like to believe that, wouldn't you, Kathie? But you know very well it's not true.

KATHIE: Yes, I know it isn't. They really detest me because of you.

JUAN: Because they think you're responsible for their father's death. Which is fair enough.

KATHIE: It's not fair enough. They never knew what happened, and they never will know either.

JUAN: They may not know the details. But they certainly smell a rat somewhere. They suspect something, they guess, they sense something. That's why they hate you and that's why you hate them.

SANTIAGO: (*Very timidly*) Did you and your husband ever separate, Kathie?

KATHIE: Johnny and I never separated . . . I . . . I was widowed.

SANTIAGO: Ah, I'd understood that . . . But what about that

gentleman I pass in the doorway of the street, or on the stairs, the one who we see in the newspapers, isn't he your husband? I'm sorry, I didn't know.

KATHIE: There's no reason why you should. Or for you to be sorry either. Aren't there thousands, millions of women in the world who have been widowed? There's nothing unusual about that.

SANTIAGO: Of course there isn't. It's as commonplace and natural as it is for a marriage to break up. (*Looks at* ANA.) Aren't there thousands, millions of women in the world who are separated from their husbands? They don't all make a Greek tragedy out of it though.

KATHIE: I'm not keen on Greek tragedy. But it turned into one in this case because Johnny darling didn't die of natural causes. Actually . . . he killed himself.

(SANTIAGO *appears not to hear her, concentrating as he is on* ANA *who has burst out laughing again.*)

SANTIAGO: Why are you laughing? Out of spite? Jealousy, is it? Envy? Or just plain stupidity?

ANA: Curiosity, professor.

SANTIAGO: Oh, go and do the cooking, clean the house, look after your daughters, do those things a woman's supposed to do in life for a change.

ANA: First, just clear up one little point for me. I'm dying to know why that pupil of yours, Adèle, left you. Ha ha ha . . .

(*African tom-tom music bursts out suddenly, as if willed by* SANTIAGO *to escape a painful memory. He quickly takes hold of the tape-recorder; he is quite stunned.*)

SANTIAGO: I've no time now, I'm very busy, the two hours are nearly up. Go away. (*Dictating*) And finally, after travelling for countless hours in the stifling heat and sweat through lush vegetation burgeoning with bamboo, ebony and breadfruit, the rickety old bus jolts to a halt in a small village between Moshe and Mombasa.

KATHIE: Then, there in a little hut we saw something quite, quite unbelievable.

SANTIAGO: (*Dictating*) Then we witness a spectacle so unimaginable that it makes our blood run cold.

KATHIE: Some little boys, completely bare, their bellies bulging out in front of them, were eating pieces of earth, as if they were sweets.

SANTIAGO: Some naked children, their stomachs swollen by parasites, were satiating their hunger with some pieces of suspiciously white-looking meat. What am I seeing? Can I believe my eyes? Petrified, I realize what these ravenous little creatures are devouring: one of them is eating a little hand, another a foot, that one over there, a shoulder, which they've torn from the carcass of another child.

KATHIE: (*Disconcerted*) Do you mean they were cannibals? (SANTIAGO *stops dictating, discouraged by* ANA's *sardonic look.*)

SANTIAGO: It gives it more of a sense of drama. It's more original, more shocking. A few children eating earth isn't going to surprise anyone, Kathie. It's something that happens here in Peru as well.

KATHIE: (*Astonished*) Here in Peru? Are you sure?

SANTIAGO: Peru isn't Lima, Kathie. And Lima isn't San Isidro. Here in this district you won't see it, but in certain less well-off areas and in a lot of places up in the mountains, what you saw in that African village is really quite common. You've been round the world twice, or three times, is it? Yet you give me the impression that you don't really know your own country properly.

KATHIE: I went to Cuzco once, with Johnny. The altitude made me feel awful. You're right, you know. Here in Peru we know more about what goes on abroad than we do about our own country. We're really such snobs!

ANA: (*Killing herself with laughter*) Yes, we are, aren't we . . . ? Particularly if we happen to be multi-millionaires. (SANTIAGO *resigned, abandons the tape-recorder and looks at* ANA.)

SANTIAGO: All right have it your own way, you spoilsport!

ANA: How ridiculous you are, Mark Griffin! You leave your wife, and your daughters, you run off with some stupid little Lolita of a girl, you make yourself the laughing stock of the entire university. And all for what? The vamp abandons you after a few weeks and you come limping home to say you're sorry with your tail between your legs. (*Very sarcastically*) Might one be allowed to know why Adèle left you, Victor Hugo?

KATHIE: (*Changed into an irate Adèle, to* SANTIAGO) Because I'm young, my life's just beginning, I want to enjoy myself. Why should I live like a nun? If I had the vocation, I'd have gone into a convent. Do you understand?

SANTIAGO: (*Contrite, intimidated*) Of course I do, my little Persian kitten. But don't exaggerate, it's not that important.

KATHIE: You know very well I'm not exaggerating. You spend the whole day telling me how desperately in love with me you are, but when it comes to the point, when it come to the actual love-making, pssst . . . you're just like a pricked balloon.

SANTIAGO: (*Trying to make her speak more quietly, to calm her, so that no one hears*) You really must try to be a little more understanding, my little Persian kitten.

KATHIE: (*Getting more and more annoyed*) You're nothing but a fake, Mark. You're all façade, a hippopotamus who looks quite terrifying but who only eats little birds.

SANTIAGO: (*Terribly uncomfortable*) I have a lot of worries, my little Persian kitten, that wretched Ana – she's constantly scheming behind my back, it nearly drives me up the wall. And then there's those lectures I'm giving at the moment on the Spanish mystics, their theories and sermons on asceticism, they really have quite a special effect on the psyche, you know, they anaesthetize the libido. Shall I explain to you what the libido is? It's very interesting, as you'll see. A gentleman called Freud . . .

KATHIE: I don't give a damn about the psyche or the libido. It's all a lot of excuses, a pack of lies, a load of rubbish. The truth is you're weak, spineless, cowardly and, and . . .

ANA: Impotent, is that the word?

133

KATHIE: That's it, that's it, impotent. That's exactly what you are, Mark Griffin: you're impotent!

SANTIAGO: (*Who doesn't know which way to turn*) Don't say that word, Adèle. And don't talk so loud, the neighbours will hear us, how embarrassing. During the holidays, when the pressure is off, you'll see how . . .

(ANA *listens to them; she's killing herself with laughter.*)

KATHIE: Do you think I'm going to wait till the summer before we next make love?

SANTIAGO: But we made love only the other night, after that film, my angel.

KATHIE: That was three weeks ago! No! A month! Do you think I'm going to saddle myself with some feeble old fuddy-duddy, who can only manage it once a month after seeing a pornographic film? Do you really think so?

SANTIAGO: (*Wanting to disappear from sight*) Passionate love, based on animal copulation, isn't everything life has to offer, my little Persian kitten. Nor is it even advisable. On the contrary, it's ephemeral, a castle made of sand which falls down at the first gust of wind. A loving relationship, on the other hand, based on mutual understanding, on a striving for common goals, ideals . . .

KATHIE: All right then, go and look for some other idiot who you can share your loving relationship with. What appeals to me is the other sort. What's it called again? Passionate love? The dirty sort, the animal sort, that's the one that interests me. *Ciao*, professor. I don't want to see you again, ever. *Ciao*, Victor Hugo!

(*She goes to applaud* JUAN, *who is showing off his prowess on the surfboard in rough waters.*)

SANTIAGO: (*Dejected, crushed, to* ANA, *who looks at him sympathetically*) You made a mountain out of a mole hill. You never had a sense of proportion, or balance between cause and effect. You can't kick someone when he's down.

ANA: No doubt another of my middle-class failings?

SANTIAGO: All marriages go through crises. The sensible thing to do is to split up without making a fuss. And make it up again later. But you had to turn the whole thing into a Greek tragedy.

ANA: It's all that education you gave me. That's probably the trouble. Weren't you the one who 'rescued' me from the middle classes? Didn't you teach me to view everything not from an individual standpoint but from a moral, social, revolutionary one? Right, when judged on that criterion you behaved abominably. (*Approaches him lovingly.*) But these are your problems, not mine. I let you go, I let you come back. We separated and we made it up again when you wanted to. I put up with you telling me all about the psyche and the libido, and your theory of love based on mutual co-operation, and the fact that you only made love to me once in a blue moon. But it really isn't my fault if you happen to like Greek tragedy, Mark Griffin.

(SANTIAGO *leans against her and* ANA *strokes his head, as if he were a little boy.*)

SANTIAGO: It's true, I'm an incorrigible romantic, but wouldn't it be nice for once in one's life to play the lead in a Greek tragedy?

(*They both look at* JUAN, *who has finished surfing and is now strutting about like a peacock: an imaginary crowd of people congratulate him and pat him on the back. He exhibits the cup he's won at the surfing championship. He looks happy and a little intoxicated.*)

JUAN: (*To* KATHIE) Why didn't you come to the party they gave for me, darling? You're never there when I need you. Everyone was asking for you and I didn't know what to say to them. Why didn't you come? It was in honour of the cup-winner, Kathie! And that cup-winner happens to be your husband! Doesn't that mean anything to you?

KATHIE: Absolutely nothing, Johnny darling. I'm fed up to the back teeth with your championships, your surfing and your celebrations. That's why I didn't go to the party and that's why I'll never go to anything to do with surfing again. Because I've never seen quite so much idiocy or quite so many idiots as I have among surfers.

JUAN: I know what the matter with you is. You're envious.

KATHIE: Of you?

JUAN: Yes, of me. Because I go in for championships and I win them. Because I'm lionized and photographed, and parties are given in my honour. Not only in Peru, but in Hawaii, Sydney and South Africa as well. Oh yes, you're envious all right. Because you're a famous little nobody, whose only claim to fame is the fact that you're my wife. That's why you knock surfing the whole time. Pure envy.

KATHIE: (*Laughing*) I quite understand why you think I'm envious of you, Johnny darling.

JUAN: And you're jealous too. Don't try and deny it! You're desperately jealous of all the young girls who are constantly coming up to me. Because there are dozens of them, hundreds of them in Lima, Hawaii, Australia and in South Africa – all feeding out of my hand.

KATHIE: It's quite true. They're bowled over just because some halfwit can keep his balance on a surfboard . . .

JUAN: And there you are – eating your heart out. The only reason you didn't go to my party was so that you wouldn't have to see all the pretty girls that were there, flirting with me. Because they're young and you're getting old. Because they're pretty and you're getting ugly. Because you're eating your heart out with jealousy.

KATHIE: Not any more. I ate my heart out to begin with. Those first few months, those first few years.

JUAN: You still do. Every time a girl takes my fancy, your face becomes all contorted, and your voice starts to quaver. Do you think I don't notice?

KATHIE: (*Lost in her memories, not hearing him*) I couldn't believe it. Every time I found you out, I nearly died. Were you with Adelita? Yes, you were. Were you with Julie? Yes, you were. With Jessie? Yes, with Jessie. With my closest friends, with my worst enemies. I felt humiliated, hurt, knocked sideways. It is true, I was eating my heart out with jealousy. I felt the world was coming to an end, I was the most helpless creature on earth. How could you go

around making love here, there and everywhere while at
the same time telling me you loved me?

JUAN: (*A little confused, trying to call a truce*) And what on earth's
that got to do with it? Love is one thing, making love
another. Of course I loved you. Don't I still? Even though
you didn't come to my party. You let me down, silly.
That's all. But all this business about making love, I've
already explained it to you: it doesn't mean anything. It
really doesn't count. I take all these girls to bed with me
and pssht, I forget about them. Like going out for a
drink, or changing my shirt. It's a physical necessity. To
keep the old dicky bird happy. I don't put my heart into
it, silly. That's reserved for you. It's like when you were
my girlfriend, remember? 'I can't go out with you tonight,
because I'm going out with a floosie.' I ask you: Whoever
heard of a girl getting jealous just because her boyfriend
goes out with a floosie? Well, it's the same thing, don't you
understand?

KATHIE: I understand perfectly. That's why I'm not jealous any
more. It wasn't out of jealousy I didn't go to your party.

JUAN: (*Conciliatory*) All right, I said that because I was in a
temper. I'm over it now. I'll let you off this time. But
just this once, mind. Don't ever play such a dirty trick on
me again. (*Smiling*) Now whisper in my ear, so that no
one can hear you, do I or do I not drive you wild with
jealousy?

KATHIE: You never drive me wild with jealousy now, Johnny
darling.

JUAN: (*Playing, and making a great show of affection*) Tell me I
do, that I drive you wild, go on, I like it. Does your little
husband drive you wild with jealousy?

KATHIE: One gets jealous when one's in love. I stopped loving
you some time ago now, Johnny darling.

JUAN: Are you being serious?

KATHIE: When I began to realize what a nonentity, what a fool
you were . . .

JUAN: Have you any idea what you're saying?

KATHIE: . . . when I saw how empty your life was, and what

137

a mess you'd made of mine. It was then I stopped being
jealous.

JUAN: So you want an argument, do you? You desert me when
I most need you and then you give yourself the luxury of
insulting me into the bargain.

KATHIE: It was when I started to despise you – then, my
jealousy began to disappear. There's not a trace of it left
now. So you can give your heart as well as your dick to all
the pretty girls you want, Johnny darling.

JUAN: Ah, it must really have hurt you, what I said. I was
ready to make it up with you, silly. We'd better talk about
something else, I'm sick and tired of hearing the same
insults over and over again. You're like a long-playing
record.

KATHIE: No, let's carry on talking about jealousy. After all,
you started it. How many times have you been unfaithful
to me? How many pretty girls have there been?

JUAN: (*Furious again*) More than you might think.

KATHIE: Twenty? Fifty? A hundred? It can't be much more
than that. (*Calculating*) Let's see now, we've been married
ten years – a hundred would make about ten a year,
practically one a month. You're right, it could be more.
How about a hundred and fifty? Two hundred?

JUAN: I had all the women I bloody well wanted.

KATHIE: You've lost count. But I haven't, Johnny darling. I
know exactly how many times I've been unfaithful to you.

JUAN: Don't play games like that, Kathie.

KATHIE: Eight, to be precise. There were even a few surfers
amongst them, just imagine. And the odd champion, I
think.

JUAN: You're not to make jokes like that, Kathie. I won't have
it.

KATHIE: There was Bepo Torres, in the summer of '57, on Kon
Tiki beach. In Bepo's little bungalow, next to the
lighthouse. His wife had taken her mother to the States,
for a facelift, remember?
(*Only now does* JUAN *appear to start believing her.*)

JUAN: Are you being serious? Are you telling the truth?

KATHIE: And then there was Ken, the Australian, the first time
we went to Sydney. Nineteen fifty-eight, wasn't it? The
one you admired so much, the one who used to get right
down into the tunnel of the wave. You were having an
affair with that friend of his, Sheila, weren't you? Well, I
had one with him, Johnny darling.
(*His consternation becomes anger, his incredulity fear.*)

JUAN: Do you want me to smash your face in? Do you want
me to kill you? What are you trying to do?

KATHIE: Then there was Kike Ricketts, the one who was mad
about cars. In 1960, in Hawaii, there was your friend
Rivarola, who used to go skin-diving. The following year,
in South Africa, there was that German we met on safari,
the one who took us to the ostrich farm in Wildemes.
Hans, whatever his name was, remember? And then last
year, there was Sapito Saldívar.
(*He puts his hand over her mouth. He seems about to strangle
her.*)

JUAN: Are you telling me the truth, you bitch?

KATHIE: (*Offering no resistance*) Don't you want to know who
the other two are?
(*He hesitates, releases her. He is sweaty, panting and
exhausted.*)

JUAN: Yes.

KATHIE: Harry Santana. And . . . Abel.

JUAN: (*Nearly out of his mind*) Abel?

KATHIE: Your brother Abel. He's the one that hurts most, isn't
he? That makes eight. (*Looks at him hard.*) Who's jealous
now?
(JUAN *is completely destroyed. He looks at* KATHIE, *stupefied.*)

JUAN: Things can't go on like this, you'll pay for this, you'll
be sorry. And those swine are going to be even more sorry
still. No, this won't do, it just won't do.
(*He sobs. He buries his face in his hands as he weeps.* KATHIE
looks on indifferently.)
Why did you do this to me?

KATHIE: (*Deeply depressed*) To get my own back for all those
pretty girls you took to bed with you under my very nose.

Because I was bored, I wanted somehow to fill the emptiness in my life. And also because I was hoping to find someone worth while, someone I could fall in love with, who could add colour to my life . . .

JUAN: You know what I'm going to do? I'm going to blow your brains out.

KATHIE: You don't have to do that, Johnny darling. It's a bit extreme. One bullet in the heart will do the trick, provided you shoot straight. I probably told you all this for that very reason. I'm sick of myself too.

JUAN: And your children? What about them?

KATHIE: Yes, I'm sick of them as well. They didn't change anything. And I'm not even interested in watching them grow up, in waiting to see what they're going to do in life. I know perfectly well already. They're going to turn into idiots, like you and me.

JUAN: You've got no feelings at all; you really are a monster.

KATHIE: I wasn't when I married you, Johnny darling. You see, I wasn't just a pretty girl. I was restless, and curious too. I wasn't just rich, I also wanted to learn, to improve myself, to do things in life. Admittedly I was rather ignorant and frivolous. But I still had time to change. You put paid to that, though. Living with you made me become like you. (*Turns towards* SANTIAGO.) I should have met you when I was young, Mark.

(*Throughout the following scene,* JUAN *gradually gets drunk.*)

SANTIAGO: Can you imagine what I was like as a young man, Kathie?

KATHIE: As clearly as if I were seeing it now.

SANTIAGO: (*In eager anticipation*) What was I like, Kathie? Tell me, please.

KATHIE: You were born in the dirty, disorderly world of the suburbs, you were an orphan and you went to a state school. You eked out a living by working as a shoeshine boy, minding cars, selling lottery tickets and newspapers.

ANA: (*Stroking his head sympathethically*) In fact you went to the Salesian Fathers. Your parents weren't poor, they just weren't very well off. Yet you didn't get a job till you were twenty.

KATHIE: You didn't go to the Catholic University, you didn't have the money, and besides, you were an atheist. So you went to the National one, to San Marcos. You were a brilliant student from the very first day. Always the first to arrive at the faculty and the last to leave. How many hours did you spend in the libraries, Mark?

SANTIAGO: A great many, a great many.

ANA: And how many playing pool in the bars on Azángaro Street? Did you ever get to the lectures on philosophy? Or Ancient History? Because you were a terrible lazybones, Mark Griffin.

KATHIE: How many books a week did Victor Hugo read? Two, three, sometimes one a day.

ANA: But you never really did much work; you'd neither the patience nor the perseverance. Did you understand Heidegger? Did you ever get round to translating a single line of Latin verse? Did you learn a foreign language?

KATHIE: As you were poor, you couldn't afford the luxuries the boys from Miraflores or San Isidro had: you'd no car, you couldn't buy yourself clothes, or become a member of the Waikiki, or go surfing, or even let your hair down on Saturdays.

ANA: And what about those beer-drinking sessions at the Patio or the Bar Palermo. Didn't that count as letting your hair down? And those visits to Señora Nanette's brothel on the Avenida Grau, which preyed so relentlessly on your socialist conscience?

KATHIE: But what did the gay social whirl of Miraflores, or the petty snobberies of San Isidro matter to Victor Hugo? His days and nights were devoted to deeper, higher things: assimilating the ideas of the great so as later to achieve greatness himself.

ANA: Why then did you abandon your studies? Why did you cheat in the exams? Why didn't you do the work? Why did you miss lectures?

KATHIE: What did you care about the feats of a few surfers on

the Pacific Ocean? For you, all that existed was the spirit,
culture and the revolution. For you also devoted your life
to stamping out social injustice, didn't you, Karl Marx?

SANTIAGO: (*Entranced*) It's true. Those Marxist study
groups . . .

ANA: . . . which bored the pants off you. Did you understand
Das Kapital? Did you ever read *Das Kapital?* Did you
finish *The Dialectic on Nature?* And what was the name of
that other book – the one with the unpronounceable title?
Materialism and Empirio something or rather?
Empirioclassicism? Empiriocriticism? Empiriocretinism?
Oh, how absurd.

SANTIAGO: (*With a melancholy smile*) And then there were the
Party militants – there weren't many of us, but we were
real diehards.

KATHIE: The militants, yes, of course. Teaching the poor to
read, forming charities, distributing alms, organizing
bazaars, strikes, revolutions, planting bombs.

ANA: You mean gossiping *ad nauseam* in university corridors,
or seedy little cafés in the centre of town. Accusing
Maoists of being Trotskyites, Leninists of being Stalinists,
socialists of being revisionists, and anyone who didn't
agree with you of being Fascists, Nazis or secret police.

KATHIE: (*Exultant*) This was life, Victor Hugo! This was youth,
Karl Marx! Culture, politics, books, charities, prisons,
revolutions, executions. Never a dull moment! You didn't
feel empty for a single second, did you?

SANTIAGO: I'd no time for that, Kathie.

KATHIE: (*Taking him by the hand*) And all those girlfriends you
had . . .

SANTIAGO: 'Girlfriend' is a petit-bourgeois expression. It's quite
inappropriate. Those of us in the Party involved in the
struggle call them comrades.

KATHIE: (*Eager, hopeful*) And your comrades, who followed
you, copied your manuscripts for you, brought you meals
in prison, supported you and co-operated with you, simply
because they were your comrades – they too became

affected and enriched by that wonderfully varied life you led, did they not?

ANA: (*Still affectionate and sympathetic*) No, they didn't. Well, they didn't, did they, Mark Griffin?

KATHIE: When you lead such a life when you're young, you go on to do great things.

(*A doubt crosses her mind. She looks at* SANTIAGO *suddenly, disconcerted.*)

And yet . . .

ANA: And yet, Mr Mark Griffin, Mr Victor Hugo, Mr Karl Marx, you still haven't done any of those great things. Why not?

SANTIAGO: (*Distressed*) Why, after all that preparation for doing great things . . .

ANA: . . . you only succeeded in doing paltry little things . . .

SANTIAGO: What happened to all those books you were going to write?

ANA: What happened to those political parties you were going to join?

SANTIAGO: What happened to all those strikes you were going to organize, those revolutions you were going to mastermind and incite?

ANA: What happened to those women you were always dreaming about, those affairs you were going to have, that life of luxury you were going to lead?

SANTIAGO: What happened to those intellectual, social and sexual *tours de force* you were going to bring off?

KATHIE: What happened, Victor Hugo?

ANA: What happened, Karl Marx?

KATHIE: What happened, Mark Griffin?

(SANTIAGO *looks to right and left, searching desperately to find an answer.*)

SANTIAGO: I married the wrong woman. She was no help to me, she never understood me. She dragged me down by her ignorance, pettiness and stupidity. That's what happened! I married a miserable idiot who thwarted me, ruined me, and finally emasculated me.

KATHIE: (*Radiantly, embracing him*) I knew it. I knew it. So it happened to you as well. We're so alike, we've so much in common. Neither of us knew how to choose. Our lives would have been so different, if we hadn't married the way we did. But isn't it wonderful we know each other, that we've so much in common, Mark?

SANTIAGO: (*Embracing her as well*) You're the comrade I should have had. You'd have understood me, you'd have been my stimulus, my strength, and my spur. I needed someone to believe in me, someone to be my bulwark against apathy and despair, someone to . . .

(*A little laugh from* ANA *forces* SANTIAGO *to look at her.*)
And I didn't just make a mistake the first time! I made one the second time too. Adèle was no help to me either, she demanded things I didn't have, or couldn't give. She upset all my values, caused havoc in my life, she humiliated me . . .

ANA: (*Pulling a face at him*) Cuckoo! Cuckoo!

SANTIAGO: That's what happened. My wife administered the poison, and my lover delivered the *coup de grâce*.

KATHIE: That's exactly what happened to me with Bepo, Ken, Kike, Rivarola, Hans, Sapito Saldívar, Harry and Abel. We didn't choose our lovers very well either, did we! None of them understood us, none of them stimulated us, inspired us or spurred us on. All they did was thwart us, ruin us and emasculate us.

SANTIAGO: (*Looking into her eyes, full of excitement*) Ah, isn't it wonderful we know each other, that we've so much in common, Kathie?

KATHIE: Then you'll rescue me from the skating rink, the barbecues and the parties, you'll deliver me from that infernal surfing.

SANTIAGO: With me, you'll read books, you'll see every exhibition, and attend every concert.

KATHIE: I'll bring food to you in prison, I'll copy out your manuscripts – for you, I'll learn to plant bombs, to kill.

SANTIAGO: We'll criticize novels, poetry and drama. You'll be my strength, my inspiration, the antidote to all my doubts. I'll read you whatever I write and you'll give me ideas, words and subjects for theses.

ANA: And who'll wash the dishes, scrub the floors and change the nappies? Who'll do the cooking?

KATHIE: Together we'll learn Chinese, Greek, and German . . .

SANTIAGO: . . . Russian, Japanese.

ANA: And will your cock crow every two months? Three months? Six months?

KATHIE: A life of love and art . . .

SANTIAGO: Revolution, and ecstasy.

KATHIE: Ah! Ah!

SANTIAGO: And when I hold you in my arms naked, we'll be like emperors in paradise.

ANA: Isn't that one of Victor Hugo's expressions?

KATHIE: I love you, I love you. Oh Mark, say you love me too.

SANTIAGO: I do, I do. And tonight my cock will crow nine times, Adèle.

(*He kisses her passionately.* ANA *laughs, but her laugh is stifled by the voice of* JUAN, *who is going back home, drunk as a lord, with a pistol in his hand.*)

JUAN: I'll kill all nine of them. First the eight samurai, then you. Then myself. Christ Almighty! Things can't go on like this. (*Catches sight of his reflection.*) What are you looking at, you cuckold? Cuckold, cuckold, cuckold. Because that's what you are, Johnny darling! A bloody great cuckold with horns like a billy-goat. A cuckold! (*His voice breaks off into a sob.*) How can I go on living? What have I ever done to you to make you behave like this, you bitch? Was it because I was a surfer? Did it exasperate you that much? And yet you have the nerve to call me a fool. Do I do anyone any harm with my surfing? What's wrong with liking the sport? Or is it preferable to get plastered, or to smoke pot, or give oneself a fix? I'm a pretty wholesome guy in case you hadn't realized. You think I'm a drunk? I drink just enough to have a good time. You think I'm a junkie? Well, I'm not. I smoke the odd fag. I roll myself a joint at times to give myself a lift. But you'd rather I was a drunk, or a drug addict or even a queer – anything but a surfer, wouldn't you, you bitch? You were envious of me, you couldn't stand the success I had, in Lima, Hawaii, South Africa, Australia. Yes, you bitch! I was riding waves nine feet, twelve feet, twenty feet high, while you were busy having it off behind my back. So you even did it with Abel. You thought I'd be really cut up about that, didn't you? Well, you're wrong, he's the one I'm least worried about, because at least with him it stays in the family. I'd have had his wife years ago if I'd wanted to. But I didn't, because she's got hair under her arms and I can't stand women who don't shave under their arms – ugh, they make me throw up! Things can't go on like this! Dear, oh dear. (*His voice breaks into another sob, as he gradually becomes more and more fuddled.*) You'll never be able to look people in the face again, Johnny darling. How are you going to walk down the street, you great cuckold, with those enormous antlers crashing into the walls and knocking people over? The weight of them will drag you to the bottom of the ocean. You can win all the championships you like now, Johnny, you can ride the most treacherous waves. But what good will it do? You're a marked man. And you'll never live this down till the day you die, even after you're dead, people will still be talking about it. Johnny. Johnny? Which Johnny do you mean? Ah yes, him. The one whose wife was always deceiving him. It's worse than original sin, worse than cancer. I'd sooner go blind, catch leprosy, or syphilis. I'd sooner burn in hell. Eight times, Johnny! What a whore! What a whore! (*Sobs.*) What if she lied to you? What if it's all a story, just to make your life a misery? She hates you, Johnny, she hates you. And do you know why? Because she's got no charm, whereas you're *simpático*, you're a real darling, you're everybody's favourite, and women go crazy about you. Why do you hate me so much, you whore? Is it because I didn't spend my life in the bank, like my old man and Abel? What on earth for? Just to make more money? What do I need more money for? I prefer to make the most of life, while it lasts. If people want to

work, let them. Let them go on coining it in, wearing themselves out. When the old man dies, I'll blow every last cent he leaves me. Just like that – in next to no time. Do you want me to waste my life, slogging my guts out so I can die a millionaire? And leave a fortune to my children – when they aren't even my children anyway? (*Sobs.*) Or are you going to try and tell me they are now, you whore! How could you, how could you! What a daft, what an idiotic thing to do – sleeping around like that just because you're jealous of my prick. None of those women ever meant anything to me, anyone would have seen that except you. I just did it to pass the time of day, I often did it out of politeness, out of consideration, I didn't want to appear rude or ungracious. You ought to feel proud of me not jealous, you bitch.
(*He's come to the end, tottering to where* KATHIE *is standing.*) I want to know right now, if my children really are my children or if in fact they belong to the eight samurai. (KATHIE *looks at him impassively, without showing the least bit of concern about Johnny's revolver.*)

KATHIE: Alexandra is yours, there's no question about that. As for little Johnny, I'm not so sure. He could be Ken the Australian's. I've always had my doubts about him. Now that's something we'll share.

JUAN: (*Tottering about, exhausted*) You're lying. Now you really are bluffing, you must be. It's all been an elaborate hoax, a joke in bad taste. All that about little Johnny and the eight samurai. You made it all up, didn't you? You invented it, just to get a rise out of me? (*His voice breaks off. He falls to his knees, imploring.*) Darling, Pussikins, for the love of God, I beg you, tell me it's not true you were unfaithful to me, tell me little Johnny is my son. I ask you on my knees, I beseech you, I'll kiss your feet. (*Drags himself along, groaning.*) Even if it is true, just say it was a lie. So at least I can go on living, Kathie.

KATHIE: (*Looking him slowly up and down*) Everything I told you is absolutely true, Johnny darling. That's something you're going to have to live with from now on. The worst of it is, I don't feel in the least bit remorseful, even when I see you in a state like this. I'm too bitter for that. Maybe I am a monster – I must be, I suppose. Because I'm not at all sorry for you, I've no pity left.

JUAN: (*Getting up with his revolver in his hand*) You'll pay for this, you bitch.

KATHIE: Aim straight. Here, at the heart. You're shaking, come closer so you don't miss. You see I won't run away, I'm not frightened. My life came to an end some time ago now. You saw to that. Do you think I mind dying? Go on, finish the job off.

(*But* JUAN *doesn't manage to fire. His hand shakes, his body shakes. He collapses at* KATHIE's *feet. He puts the revolver to his own temple and shuts his eyes. He is sweating, and trembling like a leaf. He still can't bring himself to fire.* KATHIE *now seems sympathetic.*)

If you can't kill me, with all that hatred you must have for me inside you, you certainly won't be able to kill yourself. It's harder to commit suicide than to murder someone. It takes more courage than it does to ride twenty-five-foot waves. It requires nobility of character, a sense of style, a flair for the tragic, and a romantic soul. You haven't got any of these things, Johnny darling.

JUAN: (*Sobbing, the revolver at his temple*) But you have. Help me, Pussikins, help me. After what you've done, after what you've told me, I can't go on living, knowing what I do. Help me, help me.

(*With his free hand, he makes* KATHIE *put her hand on top of his, over the trigger.*)

Go on, squeeze. Get your own back for all those things you say I've done to you. Get your own back for the surfing, for Waikiki, for all the emptiness. Now's your chance, go on, free yourself . . .

(*With a sudden decisive gesture,* KATHIE *squeezes the finger* JUAN *is holding over the trigger. The shot rings out loud, and* JUAN *rolls on the floor. Everything freezes for a few moments.*)

SANTIAGO: What do you do with yourself here in Paris, Kathie,

when you're not writing your book on the Far East and
Black Africa?

KATHIE: (*Tired and discouraged*) I go to the Louvre, the Jeu de
Paume, the Orangerie, the Grand Palais, the Museum of
Modern Art, or the galleries on the rue de Seine. I walk
for hours, I stand for hours, I get very tired and my feet
swell up. I try to make up for lost time.

SANTIAGO: (*To* ANA) She tries to make up for lost time. While
you carry on just the same as when I first met you.

ANA: I never had time to improve or be any different. We
couldn't afford a servant, what with the pittance you got
from *La Crónica*. And when you landed yourself that
teaching contract at the university, you said, 'I'm sorry,
Anita, we can't possibly have servants, my principles won't
allow it.' They didn't seem to balk at your wife becoming
one though, did they? You're right, I carry on just the
same. But what about you? Have you changed much?
Yes, I do believe you have. Are you sure it's for the better
though?   \
(*She helps* JUAN *get up and the two of them exit, arm in arm,
as if they were ghosts.*)

KATHIE: It's just that . . . all that about it never being too late
to learn – I don't believe it. Sometimes it is too late for
certain things. One has to learn to recognize them, and
enjoy them while there's still time.

SANTIAGO: Do you mean modern art? Modern music? Avant-
garde literature?

KATHIE: I mean classical art, classical music, and reactionary
literature as well. I get bored. I don't understand. I've no
critical judgement. I can't tell if a painting is good or bad.
And it's the same with music, plays and poetry. It's the
truth, Mark. I know one should never admit it to anyone
but it's true none the less.

SANTIAGO: Modern art is very obscure. You can't see the wood
for the trees. We all get lost in that particular jungle, I
assure you.

KATHIE: I'm going to let you into another secret. You know
that frivolous, meaningless world I used to inhabit? Well,

I always used to crave for something different – something
I felt I was missing, a life full of things that would satisfy
the mind. I wanted to immerse myself in the world of the
intellect, the arts, and literature. But now when I make
the effort to read or to go to exhibitions, concerts, and
lectures, I get so bored, I wonder if the artistic world
isn't basically as false and meaningless as the one I left.

SANTIAGO: We both seem to be swimming against the tide:
we're not satisfied with what we've got, and we're always
yearning for what we haven't got.

KATHIE: The worst of it is – I don't really know what I do want
any more. Maybe I'm realizing I've lost my illusions.
Could it be old age, do you suppose?

SANTIAGO: How gloomy you're becoming these days! I don't
believe a word you've been saying. If you really were that
disenchanted with life, you wouldn't be writing that book
about Black Africa and the Far East.

KATHIE: Am I really writing it? Or are you?

SANTIAGO: I'm only your scribe, I put in the full stops and the
commas and perhaps the odd adjective here and there.
But the book is entirely yours from beginning to end.
(*The alarm clock rings, indicating that two hours have passed.*)

KATHIE: Heavens, our two hours are up, and we've hardly done
any work at all. Can you stay another half-hour?

SANTIAGO: Of course I can. And I won't charge you overtime
either.

KATHIE: Bah, overtime's the least of it. A few *soles* more or less
isn't going to make any difference to Johnny. He won't
go bankrupt. He can surely spend a little bit on art, at
least.

SANTIAGO: In that case, I will charge you for the extra half-
hour and I'll take Ana out to the pictures. She's always
complaining I never go out with her.

KATHIE: So your wife is called Ana? You must introduce her
to me. Actually, there's something I've been meaning to
say to you for some time now. Don't you think it's odd
I've never invited you to the house outside working hours?

SANTIAGO: Not at all. I realize what a hectic life you lead. I

· read about it in the newspapers. Every day a dance, a
drinks party or some reception or other.

KATHIE: They're Johnny's engagements. It would look bad if
I didn't go with him. And quite honestly, it's the least I
can do, since he is so good to me. No, that's not the real
reason. You'd get very bored with him. You're both so
different. Johnny has a heart of gold. He's the kindest man
in the world, but he's also the most philistine.

SANTIAGO: He can't be that much of a philistine, to have
reached his position in life.

KATHIE: He is, he says so himself. As far as Johnny's concerned,
the arts just get in the way of doing good business.
'Culture, the arts, I leave all that to you, Pussikins, and
you leave the practicalities of life to me.' When you get
to know him, you'll see what a philistine he is.

SANTIAGO: As a matter of fact, I do know him. I've met him
several times on my way in and out of the house. He
always looks at me as if I were some strange animal. Have
you told him what sort of work I do for you?

KATHIE: Yes, but I'm sure it went in one ear and out the other.

SANTIAGO: (*Returning to the tape-recorder*) Shall we carry on then?

KATHIE: (*Pensive, doubtful*) Yes . . . On second thoughts, I
don't think I will.

SANTIAGO: You don't think you will what?

KATHIE: Ask you and your wife here for tea or supper with
Johnny and me.

SANTIAGO: As you wish. But you've already whetted my
curiosity. May one know why?

KATHIE: Don't take it the wrong way. (*Looks tenderly at the
little Parisian attic.*) But it would be like mixing oil with
water. I'm not talking about you and Johnny, though both
of you together would be like oil and water too. No, I'm
talking about myself. When I come up the little staircase
which leads to this terrace, I leave behind San Isidro,
Lima, and Peru, and I feel as if I really am entering a
Parisian attic, where one only breathes art, culture and
fantasy. I leave behind the woman with the busy social life,
the banker's wife. Because here, I am Kathie Kennety –

spinster, widow, happily married woman, saint, or mischief-maker – someone who's experienced everything life has to offer and who only lives to enrich her soul. This little corner of my life in which you play such a vital part makes all the rest bearable. You help make my dreams a reality, and my reality a dream. I don't want the two to overlap. I don't want our friendship to go beyond this little room of lies. That's why it's better if you don't meet my husband and that's why I don't want to meet your wife. I'd rather they stayed behind down below. You do understand that, don't you?

SANTIAGO: Of course I do. And I'll tell you why. Listening to you talk, I think I understand why I never felt like bringing Anita up here.

KATHIE: Have you told her about my little Parisian attic?

SANTIAGO: I told her you'd had a little playroom built on your roof. You know how inquisitive women are, she's always nagging me to bring her here to see it. It nearly drives me mad. I keep fobbing her off with the excuse you wouldn't like it, but I don't think that's the real reason at all.

KATHIE: What is the real reason?

SANTIAGO: The same as the one you gave me – to stop me meeting your husband and coming to your house – the downstairs one, I mean. Without realizing it, Kathie, I've entered into the game myself. After teasing you so mercilessly, I've let myself be captivated by this little room too.

KATHIE: I always suspected you were laughing at Kathie Kennety and her little Parisian attic.

SANTIAGO: Of course I was. I thought you were crackers – a middle-class woman with more money than sense, playing a very expensive game. I found you ridiculous. I used to believe it was just for the money you paid me that I came up here for those couple of hours each day. But that's no longer the case. For some time now, I've been enjoying the game myself: these two short hours in which lies become truths, and truths becomes lies, help me tolerate the rest of the day as well.

KATHIE: It does me good to hear you say that. It lifts a weight off my mind. I trusted you from the moment I first saw you. And I'm so glad I did. My instincts didn't let me down. Thank you, Mark, very much.

SANTIAGO: I'm the one who should be thanking you. When I come up to this little attic, I begin a new life too. I leave behind the journalist who works on *La Crónica* writing mediocre articles for an even more mediocre salary. And the second-rate little lecturer with his undistinguished pupils – yes, he stays behind as well, for up here Mark Griffin is born – author, intellectual, creative genius, visionary, innovator, arbiter of intelligence, and epitome of good taste. Here, as we work, I can have those love affairs I never really had, I can live through Greek tragedies I hope never actually to experience. And here, thanks to you, I not only travel through the Far East and Black Africa but through many other places no one would ever suspect.

KATHIE: You said mediocre – mediocrity. Isn't this a very mediocre game as well?

SANTIAGO: Maybe it is, Kathie. But at least we've still got our imagination, our ability to dream. We mustn't let anyone take that little toy away from us because it's the only one we've got.

KATHIE: How well we understand each other. And what good friends we've become.

SANTIAGO: Friends and accomplices, Kathie.

KATHIE: Yes, accomplices. That reminds me, shall we start again?

SANTIAGO: Let's. Whereabouts in Black Africa were we?
(*He returns to his tape-recorder. We hear some exotic music, a mixture of Arab and African – sensual, seductive and mysterious.*)

KATHIE: (*Looking through her papers*) Let's see now . . . On the island of Zanzibar. The small aeroplane landed at dusk.

SANTIAGO: The shadows are falling, as I alight from the little aircraft midst shrubs and coconut palms which murmur with the sounds of the island of Zanzibar, confluence of

every race, language and religion, the land of a thousand
adventures.

KATHIE: The small hotel where I had a room booked was a
ramshackle old house full of flies and Arabs.

SANTIAGO: The mystical aura of palaces, minarets and
whitewashed fortresses gradually takes hold of me, as a
coolie trots slowly through half-empty streets, pushing the
rickshaw which bears me to my lodgings – a lofty Islamic
tower which stands watch over the city.

KATHIE: I asked for a cup of tea which I gulped down, then I
did a quick change, and though the proprietress advised
me not to, I dashed out to explore the city. Its name
sounded like something out of a film.

SANTIAGO: Swarthy Swahili-speaking servants, who practise
animism, offer me a herbal potion and my exhaustion
vanishes. My strength and courage return after a Turkish
bath and a massage from native women with deft hands
and pert little breasts. Though they warn me that robbery
and rape are rife, and tell me of every sort of crime that
befall lone women in the Zanzibar night, out I go regardless
to explore the city.

KATHIE: The streets were very narrow, there was a smell of
animals and plants. Natives in local costumes were passing
by. I walked on and on until I eventually arrived at a
building that looked like a palace . . .

SANTIAGO: I lose myself in a labyrinth of narrow little lanes,
an interminable maze of steps, terraces, balconies and
stone pediments. Wild horses whinnying in the woods
serenade me, and the scent of the clove tree drives me
wild with desire. What is this building with its lattice
windows of finely carved tracery, bronze studded gates
and dancing columns? It's the sultan's palace! But I don't
even pause – I carry on forward midst beturbaned
Muhammadans, wailing beggars, hissing whores as shrill
as piccolos and ebony-skinned youths with dazzling smiles
undressing me hungrily with their eyes, until I reach a
little square, where I have a funny feeling the slave market
once was . . .

LA CHUNGA

To Patricia Pinilla

INTRODUCTION

The plot of this play can be summed up in a few sentences.

The action takes place in Piura, a city surrounded by desert in the north of Peru. In the district of the sports stadium, there is a small bar frequented by a poor and dubious clientele and run by a woman known as La Chunga. One night, Josefino, one of the regulars, comes in with his latest conquest, Meche, a slim and very attractive young woman. La Chunga is instantly captivated. Josefino, in order to amuse himself and his friends – a group of layabouts who call themselves the superstuds – goads Meche into provoking La Chunga. In the course of the night Josefino loses all his money playing dice. So that he can carry on playing, he hires out Meche to La Chunga, and the two women spend the rest of the night together in La Chunga's little room, next to the bar. After that night, Meche disappeared and has never been heard of since. What has happened between them?

The play begins some time after this event. At that same table in the bar, the superstuds, who still play dice, try in vain to find out the truth from La Chunga. They don't succeed. So they invent it. The scenes which they each dream up are brought to life on stage and maybe there is some element of fleeting truth in them. But they are, above all, secret, private truths which lie hidden in each one of them. In La Chunga's house, truth and falsehood, past and present, co-exist, as in the human soul.

The various themes the play develops or touches upon shouldn't give rise to confusion: they are love, desire, taboos, the relationship between men and women, the habits and customs of a certain milieu, the status of women in a primitive, male-dominated society, and the way in which these objective factors are reflected in the sphere of fantasy. It is clear in the play, I think, that objective reality does not condition or subdue man's desires – on the contrary, thanks to his imagination and his ambitions, even the most unsophisticated of human beings can momentarily at least break out of the prison in which he is trapped.

159

As in my two earlier plays, *The Young Lady from Tacna* and *Kathie and the Hippopotamus*, I have tried in *La Chunga* to convey through dramatic fiction the totality of human experience: actions and dreams, deeds and fantasies. The characters in the play all have two sides to them: they are both themselves and their phantom selves – creatures of flesh and blood whose destinies are conditioned by the limitations of their lives, such as poverty, marginality, ignorance, etc. – and spiritual beings who, despite the crudity and monotony of their existence, always have access to relative freedom, through recourse to fantasy – the human attribute *par excellence*.

I use the expression 'totality of human experience' to emphasize the obvious fact that a man's actions are quite inseparable from his desires and ambitions; also because the indivisibility of these two aspects of human experience should be apparent in performance, where the audience should be confronted with an integrated world in which what the characters say and what is going on in their imaginations – what actually happens and what is imagined to happen – are one continuous stream, rather like a reversible garment that can be worn either way round, so that it is impossible to tell which way round is which.

I do not see why theatre should not be a suitable medium for showing this synthesis of objective and subjective human experience, or rather, such experience in the process of synthesis. Through stubborn prejudice, however, people are inclined to think that the ambiguous, evanescent world of subtle shades and sudden arbitrary shifts, unrelated to time – the work of the imagination spurred on by desire, cannot co-exist on stage with objective reality, without creating insurmountable difficulties for the director. I do not believe there is any explanation for this scepticism other than idleness, and a fear of taking risks, without which all creative enterprise is hampered.

It is simply a question of finding a form of theatre that capitalizes on what is unique to the theatre, man's talent for pretending, for play-acting, for putting himself into situations and projecting himself into characters different from his own. In the scenes in which they act out their fantasies, the characters should be indulgent to themselves, love themselves, as they play these extensions of their own personalities, dividing themselves, as actors do when they go on stage, or as men and women do mentally when they call on their imaginations to enrich their lives, illusorily acting out those roles which are either denied them in real life, or which they seldom have a chance to play.

Finding a technique for theatrical expression – a means of realizing this practice so universally shared, that of enriching life through the creation of images and the telling of stories – ought to be a stimulating challenge for those who want a new kind of theatre or who want to explore new avenues, rather than painfully pursuing those three archetypes of modern theatre which are already starting to show signs of ossification from over-use: the epic didacticism of Brecht; the pure entertainment value of the theatre of the absurd; and the affected spontaneity of the happening and other variations on the improvised show. The theatre and the images it can create are, I'm sure, an ideal medium for the expression of that tangled and disturbing world of angels, demons and wonders which lie at the heart of our desires.

Mario Vargas Llosa

CHARACTERS

LA CHUNGA
MECHE

The superstuds
EL MONO
JOSE
JOSEFINO
LITUMA

LA CHUNGA'S HOUSE

Piura, 1945.

La Chunga's restaurant-bar is near the stadium, in a district of
reed matting and wooden planks which grew up not long ago
in the sandy area, between the main road to Sullana and the
Grau Barracks. Unlike the flimsy dwellings of the
neighbourhood, it is a proper building – with adobe walls and
zinc roof – spacious and square. On the ground floor there are
rustic tables, benches and seats where customers sit, and a
wooden counter. Behind this, there is a kitchen, blackened
and smoky. On a higher level, which is reached by a small
staircase, there is a room, which no customer has ever visited.
It is the proprietress's bedroom. From there, La Chunga can
observe all that goes on below through a window hidden
behind a flower-patterned curtain.

The customers of the little bar are local people, soldiers from
the Grau Barracks on leave, football fans and boxing
enthusiasts, stopping for a drink on their way to the stadium,
or workers from the building site in that new area for the rich
which is making Piura into an expanding city: it is called Buenos
Aires.

La Chunga has a cook who sleeps in front of the stove, and
a boy who comes in during the day to serve at the tables. But
she is always at the bar – usually standing. When there are not
many customers, as tonight, when the only people in the place
are those four layabouts who call themselves the superstuds
(they have been playing dice and drinking beer for some time)
La Chunga can be seen rocking slowly back and forth in a
rocking chair made of reeds, which creaks monotonously, as
she gazes into space. Is she lost in her memories or is her mind
a blank – is she simply existing?

She is a tall, ageless woman, with a hard expression, smooth
taut skin, strong bones and emphatic gestures. She observes
her customers with an unblinking gaze. She has a mop of black
hair, tied back with a band, a cold mouth and thin lips – she
does not speak much and she rarely smiles. She wears short-

sleeved blouses and skirts so unseductive, so unprovocative,
that they seem like the uniform of a school run by nuns.
Sometimes she goes barefoot, sometimes she wears heel-less
sandals. She is an efficient woman: and runs the place with an
iron hand and knows how to command respect. Her physical
appearance, her air of severity, her terseness, are intimidating;
it's not often that drunks try to take liberties with her. She
does not listen to confidences nor does she accept compliments;
she has never been known to have a boyfriend, a lover, or even
friends. She seems resolved always to live alone, dedicated body
and soul to her business. Except for that very brief episode
with Meche – which was quite baffling for the customers – no
one has ever known her altering her routine for anyone or
anything. For as long as the local Piuranos can remember, she
has only ever been seen behind the bar – where she stands
motionless and unsmiling. Does she perhaps occasionally go to
the Variedades or the Municipal to see a film? Does she take
a walk through the Plaza de Armas in the afternoon when
there's a concert? Does she go to the Eguiguren Pier or the
Old Bridge to bathe in the river at the beginning of each summer
if it has rained in the Cordillera? Does she watch the military
procession on Independence Day, among the crowd congregated
at the foot of the Grau Monument?

She is not an easy woman to engage in conversation; she
replies in monosyllables or by nodding or shaking her head
and if she is asked a facetious question she'll reply with a coarse
remark or a monstrous lie. 'La Chunguita', say the Piuranos,
'does not stand any nonsense.'

The superstuds, who are always playing dice, drinking toasts
to each other and joking, know this very well. Their table is
right underneath a kerosene lamp which hangs from a beam,
around which insects flutter. They remember the time when
the little bar belonged to a certain Doroteo, who was La
Chunga's first business associate and whom – according to
local gossip – she pushed out by hitting him over the head with
a bottle. But despite coming here twice or three times a week,
not even the superstuds could call themselves friends of La

Chunga. They are merely acquaintances, customers – nothing more. Who in Piura could boast they know her intimately? The fugitive Meche, perhaps? La Chunga has no friends. She is a shy and solitary soul, like one of those cacti in the desert of Piura.

Truth is rarely pure and never simple.

Oscar Wilde

This translation of *La Chunga* was first performed as a rehearsed reading on 29 April 1989 at the Gate Theatre, Notting Hill. The cast was as follows:

LA CHUNGA	Valerie Sarruf
MECHE	Geraldine Fitzgerald
EL MONO	Tom Mannion
JOSE	John Skitt
JOSEFINO	Tom Knight
LITUMA	Alan Barker
Director	David Graham-Young

ACT ONE

A game of dice

EL MONO: (*Holding the dice above his head*) Come on,
superstuds. Let's sing the old song again, to bring me
some luck.

JOSE, LITUMA, JOSEFINO *and* EL MONO (*Sing in chorus with
great gusto*)

We are the superstuds.
We don't want to work.
All we want is a little bit of skirt.
Drinking, gambling all night long,
In Chunga's bar where we belong.
Wine, women and song –
Wine, women and song.
In Chunga's bar where we belong.
In Chunga's bar where it's cheap and nice,
And now we're going to throw the dice!

(EL MONO *blows on his fist and kisses it, then throws the dice
on to the table. The little black and white cubes hurtle across
the top of the table, bouncing up and down, colliding,
ricocheting off the half-empty glasses and finally come to rest,
their journey cut short by a bottle of Cristal beer.*)

EL MONO: Ahaha! Two threes! That'll do me nicely. Right, I'm
doubling the bank.

(*No one reacts or adds a single cent to the pool of banknotes
and coins that* EL MONO *has beside his glass.*)

Well come on, you spineless lot of buggers. Is no one going
to take me on?

(*He picks up the dice, cradles them in his hands, blows on
them and shakes them above his head.*)

Now here goes for another six – a five and a one, a four
and a two, a three and a three – or this little stud's going
to chop off his pecker.

JOSEFINO: (*Offering him a knife*) For all the use it is – here,
borrow my knife. Go on, cut it off!

JOSE: Just toss the dice, will you, Mono. It's about the one
thing you're good at – tossing.

EL MONO: (*Pulling faces*) And they're off . . . Whoosh. A three
and a six. (*Crosses himself.*) Holy Whore. Now for the six.

LITUMA: (*Turning towards the bar*) Don't you think Mono's
become very vulgar lately, Chunga?

(LA CHUNGA *remains unperturbed. She does not even deign to
glance at the superstuds' table.*)

JOSE: Why don't you answer poor Lituma, Chunguita? He's
asking you a question, isn't he?

EL MONO: She's probably dead. That thing rocking backwards
and forwards over there is most likely her corpse. Hey,
Chunga, are you dead?

LA CHUNGA: You'd like that, wouldn't you? So you could
scarper without paying me for the beers.

EL MONO: Ahaha. I've brought you back to life again, Chunga,
Chunguita. (*Blows on the dice, kisses them, and throws
them.*) Holy Whore. Now for the six.

(*All four of them watch, their eyes glued to the little black and
white cubes as they go on their bumpy journey among glasses,
bottles, cigarettes and matchboxes. This time they roll off the
table on to the wet earthen floor.*)

One and three is four, superstuds. I just needed another
two. The bank is still up – if anyone's got the balls to
bet.

LITUMA: Hey, what happened that time with Meche, Chunga?
Go on. Make the most of it while it's just us today. Tell
us.

JOSE: Yes, go on, tell us, Chunguita.

LA CHUNGA: (*Detached as always, in a drowsy voice*) Go and ask
your bloody mother. She'll tell you.

(EL MONO *throws the dice.*)

EL MONO: And it's a six! Right, you bastards, I'm pissing on
you all from a very great height. Now open your mouths
and start swallowing, hahaha! (*Turns towards the bar.*) It
must be your sweet temper, bringing me luck, Chunguita.
(*Lifts up the kitty and kisses the banknotes and coins in an*

extravagant manner.) Another couple of beers, nice and cold mind – because this time, they're on me! Hahaha!

(LA CHUNGA *gets up. The chair carries on rocking, creaking at regular intervals, as she, the owner of the bar, goes to fetch a couple of bottles of beer from a bucket full of ice, which she keeps beneath the bar. Listlessly, she carries them to the superstuds' table and places them in front of* EL MONO. *The table is bristling with bottles.* LA CHUNGA *returns to the rocking chair.*)

JOSE: (*Provocatively, in a shrill voice*) Are you never going to tell us what you did that night with Meche, Chunga?

JOSEFINO: Do you want to be raped? Well, shut up about Mechita, d'you hear, or I'll have the pants off one of you in next to no time. Just mention her name and I start to get a hard-on.

EL MONO: (*Winking, he talks in a falsetto voice*) You too, Chunguita?

LA CHUNGA: That'll do, you bastard. I'm here to serve beer, not to be made a fool of – not by anyone. Why should I listen to your smut? Just watch it, Mono.

(EL MONO *starts to tremble; his teeth start to chatter, he shows the whites of his eyes, he moves his shoulders and hands, as if in the throes of some hysterical convulsion.*)

EL MONO: Oh, I'm scared. I'm scared.

(*Helpless with laughter, the superstuds slap him to bring him to his senses.*)

LITUMA: Take it easy, Chunga. We may make you mad at times, but we love you really. You know that.

JOSEFINO: Whose bloody stupid idea was it to talk about Meche? It was you, wasn't it, Lituma? Shit, you've made me all nostalgic. (*Raises his glass, solemnly.*) Let's drink to the tastiest little wench that ever set foot this side of the Andes. To you, Mechita, in heaven, in Lima, in hell, or wherever the fuck you are.

Meche

As JOSEFINO *proposes the toast and the superstuds drink*, MECHE *enters. She moves slowly and rhythmically which suggests someone entering the real world from the world of the memory. She is young and neat and has a firm, full figure – very feminine. She wears a light, close-fitting dress, and shoes with stiletto heels. She cuts quite a dash, as she walks.* LA CHUNGA'*s eyes widen and light up, as she watches her approach, but the superstuds remain unaware of her presence. By comparison,* LA CHUNGA'*s attention is focused on her so intensely that it is almost as if the present were losing all concrete reality for her, as if it were becoming blurred, fading away, to the point of extinction. Even the voices of the superstuds become thinner and fainter.*

EL MONO: I'll never forget the look on your face that time Meche came in here, Chunguita. Quite stunned, you were.

LITUMA: You're the only one who knows where she is, Chunga. Come on, do us a favour. What's it to you? Put us out of our misery.

JOSE: No. Why don't you tell us what happened that night between the pair of you, Chunguita? Shit, I can't bloody sleep at night for thinking about it.

EL MONO: I'll tell you what happened.

(*Sings, pulling his usual funny faces:*)
Chunga with Meche
Meche with Chunga
Cheche with Menga
Menga with Cheche
Chu Chu Chu
And long live Fumanchu!

LA CHUNGA: (*In a faint and distant voice; mesmerized by* MECHE, *who is now beside her*) Hurry up and empty those glasses now, I'm closing.

(*Imperceptibly,* JOSEFINO *gets up, and, moving out of the present into the past, out of reality into the world of the*

imagination, he goes and positions himself next to MECHE,
taking hold of her arm in a proprietorial fashion.)

JOSEFINO: Good evening, Chunguita. May I introduce Meche?

MECHE: (*Stretching out her hand to* LA CHUNGA) Pleased to meet
you, señora.

(*The superstuds, still engrossed in their game of dice,
acknowledge* JOSEFINO *and* MECHE *with a wave of the
hand.*)

(LA CHUNGA *holds* MECHE's *hand and devours her with her
eyes; it is clear from her voice she has been moved by the
experience.*)

LA CHUNGA: So you're the famous Meche. Welcome. I didn't
think he was ever going to bring you. I've been so much
wanting to meet you.

MECHE: So have I, señora. Josefino talks a lot about you. (*With
a gesture towards the table*) They all do, the whole time.
About you and this place. I was dying to come. (*Indicating*
JOSEFINO) But he wouldn't bring me.

(LA CHUNGA *resigns herself to releasing* MECHE's *hand; she
attempts to regain her composure and appear natural.*)

LA CHUNGA: I can't think why. I haven't eaten anyone yet to
my knowledge. (*To* JOSEFINO) Why wouldn't you bring
her?

JOSEFINO: (*Joking obscenely*) I was afraid you might take her
away from me, Chunguita. (*Putting his arm round* MECHE's
waist and flaunting her conceitedly) She's worth her weight
in gold, wouldn't you say?

LA CHUNGA: (*Admiring her and nodding*) Yes. This time I must
congratulate you, Don Juan. Even though you are from
the Gallinacera. She's worth more than all those other
women of yours put together.

MECHE: (*Rather embarrassed*) Thank you, señora.

LA CHUNGA: Don't be so formal. Just call me Chunga.

LITUMA: (*Calling from the table*) We're starting another game,
Josefino. Are you coming?

JOSE: You may as well, Josefino. It's Mono's turn with the dice.
You can guarantee it'll be a walkover with this poor cretin.

EL MONO: Me a cretin? Holy Whore, I'll be buggered if I don't fleece the lot of you before the night's out. You'll have to leave me Mechita, as a pledge, against all that money you're going to lose, Josefino.

JOSEFINO: (*To* LA CHUNGA) How much do you think I could get for this little doll, Chunguita?

LA CHUNGA: As much as you want. It's true. She is worth her weight in gold. (*To* MECHE) What are you drinking? It's on the house. Would you like a beer? A vermouth?

JOSEFINO: I don't believe it . . . Did you hear that, studs? Chunga's paying.

LA CHUNGA: Not for you, I'm not. You're a regular. I'm inviting Meche, since it's her first time here. So that she'll come back.

(*There is a great uproar from the superstuds' table.*)

EL MONO: (*Shouting*) Hahaha. Am I hearing right?

JOSE: Ask her for a whisky, and share it out, Mechita.

JOSEFINO: (*Moving towards the table to take his place again among the superstuds*) Right. I'll try my hand again.

MECHE: Weren't you going to take me to the pictures?

JOSEFINO: Later. First I'm going to make myself a few bucks by fleecing these three morons. The night's still young, pussycat.

MECHE: (*To* LA CHUNGA, *indicating* JOSEFINO) We're not going to get to the pictures tonight, I can see that. There's one on at the Variedades with Esther Williams and Ricardo Montalbán and it's in colour. With bullfighting and music. It's a pity Josefino likes gambling so much.

LA CHUNGA: (*Handing her the vermouth, which she has been preparing*) That one's into all the vices. He's the most unscrupulous bastard out. Whatever did you see in him? What do women see in such a bum? Tell me, Meche. What is it about him?

MECHE: (*Partly embarrassed, partly feigning embarrassment*) Well, he's got . . . he's a real charmer. He knows how to say nice things to a girl. And besides, he's good-looking, don't you think? And also . . . Well, when he kisses me and touches me, I start to tremble all over. I see little stars.

LA CHUNGA: (*With a mocking smile*) Does he really make you see little stars?

MECHE: (*Laughing*) Well, it's just a manner of speaking really. If you know what I mean.

LA CHUNGA: No. I don't know what you mean. I can't understand how a pretty girl like you can fall in love with a poor sod like that. (*Very seriously*) You know what'll happen to you, if you stay with him, don't you?

MECHE: I never think about the future, Chunga. You've got to take love as it comes. It's living for the moment that counts. You've got to get as much as you can out of it while it lasts. (*Becoming alarmed suddenly*) What will happen to me if I stay with him?

LA CHUNGA: He'll make you see little stars for a little while longer. And then, he'll put you into the Casa Verde – so that you can keep him, in style, by whoring.

MECHE: (*Scandalized*) What are you saying? You're joking, aren't you? Do you think I could do such a thing? You obviously don't know me. Do you really think I'm capable of . . .

LA CHUNGA: Of course I do. Like all those other silly girls who saw little stars, whenever that pimp so much as looked at them. (*Stretches out her hand and strokes* MECHE's *cheek.*) Don't look so frightened. I like you better when you smile.

The Gallinacera versus the Mangachería

At the superstuds' table, the game starts to heat up. The atmosphere is becoming electric.

EL MONO: (*Highly excited*) Three and four, seven, hahaha. So I was a cretin, was I, José? Down, on your knees and start praying, you pathetic creep. Have you ever seen anything like that in all your born days? Seven games on the trot without a single miss. The money's still all there, for the real men. Anyone take me on?

JOSEFINO: (*Taking out a few banknotes*) I will. You think you frighten me? Let's see, how much is there? Two hundred, three hundred. Here's three hundred. Come on, throw the dice, you peasant.

JOSE: That's a lot of money, Josefino. (*Lowering his voice*) You haven't by any chance been putting Mechita out to work already, have you?

JOSEFINO: Shut it, if she hears you she'll start getting all suspicious. Well, what are you waiting for, Mono?
(EL MONO *passes the dice across his eyes, then across his lips, cradles them in his hands, as if casting a spell on them.*)

EL MONO: Just making you squirm a bit, slum boy. And now here we go for real . . .
(*They all watch the dice ecstatically.*)
Eleven. There you are. This time I've really rammed it right down your throats. Eight on the trot. Let's drink to that, for Christ's sake. More beers, Chunga. We've got a minor miracle here to celebrate.
(JOSEFINO *checks* EL MONO, *as he is about to collect the money he's won.*)

JOSEFINO: The money stays on the table.
(*The three superstuds look at him in amazement.*)

EL MONO: If you want to carry on losing? Be my guest, mate. Go on, make yourself rich then, if you can. The money's there. All six hundred *sols* of it. Anyone else betting?

JOSEFINO: No just me.
(*He takes more money out of his pocket, counts it ostentatiously, places it slowly and theatrically in the kitty.*)
There you are. Six hundred. The Gallinacera versus the Mangachería.

LITUMA: Holy shit, he must have robbed a bank or something.

JOSEFINO: We leave that sort of thing to street arabs like you; we may be scavengers, in the Gallinacera, but we're not thieves.

JOSE: Don't kid yourself, Josefino. It's the worst district in Piura.

LITUMA: What with the slaughterhouse and the carcasses all over the road, and the flies and the vultures – I wouldn't brag about it too much, if I were you.

JOSEFINO: At least we've got tarmac streets and toilets. You lot haven't even got that. Nothing but donkeys and beggars. Everyone shits on the floor beside the bed. I don't know why I have anything to do with people like you. Any day now I'll even start to smell like you into the bargain. Hold it, Mono, don't throw those dice yet. Mechita, here, come and bring me some luck.

(MECHE *approaches the table, at the same time as* LA CHUNGA, *who is carrying two more beers;* JOSEFINO *puts his arm round* MECHE's *waist and kisses her salaciously and ostentatiously on the mouth, forcing her to lower her face. The superstuds laugh, drink and applaud.* LA CHUNGA *looks on, her eyes shining.*)

Right, Mono. Now throw those dice.

JOSE: (*To* JOSEFINO) You know what they say, don't you? Lucky in love, unlucky at cards.

EL MONO: (*Throwing the dice*) There they go, and this little superstud's a rich man.

JOSEFINO: (*Happy, exuberant*) Two ones. Start to dig your grave, Mono. (*To* JOSE) You've got the wrong saying, mate. It's 'Lucky in love, luckier at cards'. Here's to Mechita for bringing me such good fortune. Thank you, my little one.

(*He forces her to lower her head again and kisses her. In doing so, he looks askance at* LA CHUNGA *as if making fun of her.*)

Cheers, Chunguita.

(LA CHUNGA *doesn't answer him. She goes back to the bar.*)

EL MONO: (*Stretching out his hand to* JOSEFINO) I must congratulate you. It takes guts to bet the whole bank after eight straight runs. You may be from the Gallinacera, but you certainly deserve to be a superstud.

JOSE: (*Mischievously*) Did you see Chunga's face when Josefino was kissing you, Mechita? Her eyes were popping out of her head.

LITUMA: She was dying of envy.

JOSEFINO: (*Raising his voice*) Do you hear what these buggers are saying about you, Chunga?

LA CHUNGA: What?

JOSEFINO: That when I was kissing Meche, your eyes were popping out of your head. That you were dying of envy.

LA CHUNGA: They're probably right. Who wouldn't feel envious of a woman like that?

(*Laughter and shouting from the superstuds.*)

JOSEFINO: And you haven't even seen her in the buff, Chunguita. Her body's even better than her face. Isn't that right, Meche?

MECHE: Be quiet, Josefino.

LA CHUNGA: I've no doubt for once in your life you're telling the truth.

JOSEFINO: Of course I am. Lift up your skirt, love. Show her your legs, just to give her an idea.

MECHE: (*Pretending to be more embarrassed than she is*) Oh, Josefino, the things you say.

(JOSEFINO *speaks with an assurance that shouldn't be brusque, but which barely conceals his superiority. He relishes his authority in front of his friends.*)

JOSEFINO: (*Raising his voice a little*) Listen to me. If you and I aren't going to fall out with each other, you'd better do what I say. Show her your legs.

MECHE: (*Pretending to protest, though in fact enjoying the game*) You're so moody and bossy at times, Josefino.

(*She lifts up her skirt and shows her legs. The superstuds cheer.*)

JOSEFINO: (*Laughing*) What do you think of them, Chunga?

LA CHUNGA: Not bad.

JOSEFINO: (*Bristling with arrogance*) You see. I could make her strip stark naked in front of you and nothing would happen – because you're my mates. We trust each other, eh Chunga?

(*He begins to gather up the money he's just won from the pool.*)

EL MONO: Hold it. Only cowards draw their money out while there are people still keen to play.

JOSEFINO: You want to go for the bank? It's one thousand, two hundred *sols*, Mono. Have you got it?

(EL MONO *searches his pockets, takes out all the money he has and counts it.*)

EL MONO: I've got five hundred. I'll owe you the seven hundred.

JOSEFINO: You can't borrow money in the middle of a game, it's bad luck. (*Gripping him by the wrist*) Wait. That's what your watch is for. I'll take it instead of the seven hundred.

LITUMA: Your watch is worth more than that.

EL MONO: (*Taking off his watch, and putting it with his five hundred sols in the pool*) But I'm going to win, aren't I, for God's sake? All right, Josefino, throw those dice and please . . . lose.
(JOSEFINO *pushes* MECHE *towards the bar.*)

JOSEFINO: Go and keep Chunga company. I'm going to win that money and the watch, you'll see. With the dice in my hand, I don't need you to bring me luck, I make my own luck.

JOSE: Be careful Chunga doesn't try to seduce you, Mechita. You've almost driven her crazy.

MECHE: (*Revealing a somewhat morbid curiosity, in a whisper*) Is she one of those?

LITUMA: We didn't know she was till now. We thought she was probably sexless.

JOSE: But ever since she saw you, she's completely lost her cool. She's given herself away: she's a dike.

MECHE: Is she really?

JOSEFINO: Ears burning, are they, Chunga? If you knew what they were saying about you, you'd brain the lot of them – you'd never let them set foot in here again.

LA CHUNGA: What are they saying?

JOSEFINO: José says you've gone all crazy since you saw Mechita, he says that you've given yourself away, that you're a dike and Meche wants to know if it's true or not.

MECHE: It's a lie, Chunga, don't believe him. You are a bastard, Josefino.

LA CHUNGA: Let her come and ask me. I'll tell her in private.
(*The superstuds laugh and joke.*)

JOSEFINO: (*To* MECHE) Go on, my little one. Flirt with her a little, give her a thrill.

EL MONO: Are you going to throw those dice, Josefino?
(MECHE *goes towards the bar where* LA CHUNGA *is standing.*)

WOMEN AND DIKES

MECHE: (*Confused*) Surely you didn't believe him, did you? You know Josefino's always joking. I didn't say that about you. Really.

LA CHUNGA: Oh, don't worry. I don't give a damn what people say about me. They can say what they like. (*Shrugs her shoulders*). If that's what amuses them, then let them. Just so long as I don't hear.

MECHE: Don't you care if they say nasty things about you?

LA CHUNGA: The only thing I care about is that they don't fight and they pay for what they drink. Provided they behave and don't try and cheat me, they can say what they damned well like.

MECHE: Don't you even care if they say you're . . . that?

LA CHUNGA: A dike? (*Takes hold of* MECHE's *arm*.) And what if I were? Am I frightening you?

MECHE: (*With a nervous little laugh; we are not sure whether she means what she says or not.*) I don't know. I've never met a real dike before. I know there are supposed to be so many about, but I've never seen a single one. (*Looks* LA CHUNGA *over.*) I always imagined them to be butch and ugly. You're not like that at all.

LA CHUNGA: What am I like?

MECHE: A little hard perhaps. But I imagine you have to be to run a place like this what with all the drunks and strange types that come in. But you're not ugly. If you tidied yourself up a bit, you'd look quite attractive, beautiful even. Men would like you.

LA CHUNGA: (*With a dry little laugh*) I'm not interested if men like me or not. But you are, aren't you? It's the one thing in life that you care about, isn't it? Tidying yourself up, putting on make-up, making yourself look pretty. Anything to excite them, to titillate them. Isn't that it?

MECHE: Surely that's just being a woman?

LA CHUNGA: No. That's being an idiot.

MECHE: Then all women are idiots.

LA CHUNGA: Most of them are. That's why they get what they

deserve. They let themselves be abused, they become
slaves. For what? To be thrown on the rubbish tip like
cast-off rags when their men get tired of them.
(*Pause. She strokes* MECHE's *face again.*)
I hate to think what might happen to you when Josefino
gets tired of you.

MECHE: He'll never get tired of me. I'll always know how to
keep him happy.

LA CHUNGA: Yes. I've noticed. By letting him twist you round
his little finger. Aren't you ashamed to let him boss you
around like that?

MECHE: I enjoy doing whatever he asks me to do. For me,
that's love.

LA CHUNGA: So you'd do anything that poor sod asked you to
do?

MECHE: For as long as I'm in love with him, yes. Anything.
(*Pause.* LA CHUNGA *watches her in silence. She reveals, in
spite of herself, a certain admiration for her. They are both
distracted by the row the superstuds are making.*)

A pledge

EL MONO: (*Euphorically, gathering fistfuls of banknotes in his
hands*) Jesus Christ. This is classic. Pinch me somebody,
for heaven's sake, so I know I'm not dreaming.

JOSE: (*Giving* JOSEFINO *a slap on the back*) The game hasn't
finished yet, Mono. Leave the money on the table.

EL MONO: What are you going to go on betting with? You've
already lost two thousand *sols*, your watch and your pen.
What more have you got, for Christ's sake?
(*Pause.* JOSEFINO *looks from one side to the other. He watches*
LA CHUNGA *and* MECHE *for a moment. Then, resolutely, he
gets to his feet.*)

JOSEFINO: I have got something more.
(*He strides firmly towards* LA CHUNGA. *He has the expression
of a man prepared to go to any length to satisfy his whim.*)
I need three thousand *sols* to stay in the game, Chunguita.

LA CHUNGA: Over my dead body! You know perfectly well I
  never lend a cent to anyone.
JOSEFINO: I've got something worth more than those three
  thousand *sols* I'm asking you for.
  (*He grips* MECHE *round the waist.*)
MECHE: (*Taking it half as a joke, without knowing quite how to
  react*) What are you saying?
  (LA CHUNGA *bursts out laughing.* JOSEFINO *remains very
  serious. The superstuds have gone quiet; they crane their necks
  forward, intrigued by what is happening.*)
JOSEFINO: (*Holding* MECHE *against him as if he owned her*) You
  heard. You love me, don't you? And I love you too.
  That's why I'm asking this of you. Didn't you swear you'd
  always do anything I wanted? Right then, now you're
  going to prove it to me.
MECHE: (*Open-mouthed and incredulous*) But, but . . . have you
  gone mad? Do you know what you're saying? Or have
  those beers gone to your head?
JOSEFINO: (*To* LA CHUNGA) You can't fool me, Chunga. I know
  you've been drooling over Meche ever since you first set
  eyes on her. So what about it?
EL MONO: Holy shit. He means it. D'you realize, superstuds?
JOSE: Christ, he's selling her to her. It's as simple as that.
LITUMA: You might as well buy her yourself, Mono. Or isn't
  Mechita worth those three thousand *sols*?
JOSEFINO: (*Without taking his eyes off* LA CHUNGA; *still with his
  arm round* MECHE) No. I wouldn't lend her to Mono, not
  for all the tea in China. Nor to any other man, for that
  matter. (*Kissing* MECHE) It would make me jealous. I'd
  rip the guts out of anyone who so much as laid a finger on
  her. (*To* LA CHUNGA) But I'm not jealous of you. I'll lend
  her to you all right, because I know that you'll give her
  back to me – intact.
MECHE: (*Snivelling, bewildered and exasperated*) Let go of me. I
  want to get out of here. You miserable sod. You miserable
  sod.
JOSEFINO: (*Letting go of her*) You can go. But don't ever come
  back. Because if you go now, Meche, you'd be betraying

me. I'd never forgive you for letting me down when I most
needed you.

MECHE: But, Josefino, do you realize what you're asking me to
do? What do you think I am?

LA CHUNGA: (*To* MECHE, *sardonically*) You see, so you wouldn't
just do anything that crook asked you, after all.

JOSEFINO: (*Clutching* MECHE) Did you really say that? Did you?
Then it is true. (*Kisses* MECHE.) I love you, Meche. You
and I will always be together, for as long as we both live.
Don't cry, silly. (*To* LA CHUNGA) Well, what about it
then?

(LA CHUNGA *has become very serious. Long pause.*)

LA CHUNGA: Let her say it herself, in her own words, that she
accepts. Let her say that from now until the first light of
dawn she'll do anything I want.

JOSEFINO: (*To* MECHE) Don't let me down. I need you. She
won't do anything to you. She's a woman. What can she
do to you? Say it.

(*Trance-like pause. The superstuds and* LA CHUNGA *watch*
MECHE's *inner conflict. She stretches out her arms and looks
from one to the other.*)

MECHE: (*To* LA CHUNGA, *stammering*) I'll do anything you want
until the first light of dawn.

(LA CHUNGA *goes to fetch the money from under the bar.*
JOSEFINO *whispers something into* MECHE's *ear and caresses
her. The superstuds start to recover from the shock.* LA CHUNGA
hands the money to JOSEFINO.)

EL MONO: Bloody hell, I really don't believe this. I don't believe
my eyes.

LITUMA: I could even marry a woman like that.

JOSE: Shit. This calls for us to sing the old song again. For
Mechita. She deserves it.

EL MONO: The song, superstuds – and a toast in honour of
Mechita.

EL MONO, LITUMA *and* JOSE: (*Singing*)
    We are the superstuds.
    We don't want to work.
    All we want is a little bit of skirt.

Drinking, gambling all night long,
In Chunga's bar where we belong.
Wine, women and song –
Wine, women and song.
In Chunga's bar where we belong.
And now we're going to drink a toast
To you, Mechita.'

(They raise their beer glasses to MECHE *and drink.* LA CHUNGA *takes* MECHE *by the hand and leads her towards her room. They both go up the small staircase.* JOSEFINO, *counting his money, returns to the gambling table.)*

ACT TWO

The superstuds

As the curtain goes up, the actors are in exactly the same position as they were at the beginning of the first act. We are now in the present – a long time after the episode with MECHE. *The superstuds are playing dice at the table, beneath a lamp which is hanging from a beam, while* LA CHUNGA, *in her rocking chair, passes the time by gazing into space. In the coolness of the night, the sounds of the city can be heard in the distance: crickets chirp, there is the occasional noise of a car, a dog barks, a donkey brays.*

JOSE: I'm dying to know what Chunga did that night with Meche; how much do you think it would take to get her to tell me?

LITUMA: She'll never tell you. Not even for a million *sols*. Forget it, José.

JOSEFINO: If I wanted her to, she would. For free.

EL MONO: We know what a naughty boy you are, Josefino, you great crook.

JOSEFINO: I'm not joking. (*Takes out his knife and holds it so that it glints in the light of the lamp.*) Chunga may be pretty tough, but there's no man or woman alive who wouldn't squeal like a parrot with this at his throat.

EL MONO: D'you hear that, Chunga?

LA CHUNGA: (*With her usual detachment*) Hurry up and finish those beers. I'm about to close.

JOSEFINO: Don't be frightened, Chunguita. I'd make you tell me what happened that night if I felt like it. But I don't feel like it. So you can stuff your little secret. I don't want to know. I don't give a damn about Meche. She could be dead for all I care. I've yet to meet the woman who'd make me run after her.

(JOSE *has stood up. He moves slowly towards* LA CHUNGA's *rocking chair, staring straight ahead of him, gaping slightly, as if walking in his sleep. The superstuds appear not to have noticed him. Throughout the following scene, they behave as*

185

if he were still sitting in the empty seat: they clink glasses with
him, take his bets, pass him the dice, slap him on the back
and joke with him.)

JOSE: (*His voice is dry and feverish*) Nobody knows about it,
Chunga, but something in my life changed that night.
(*Hits himself on the head.*) I can still see it all, as if it were
happening now. Everything you said and everything
Meche said – I remember it all so very clearly. When you
took her by the arm and led her over there, to your room,
my heart was beating so hard, I thought it would leap out
of my chest. (*Takes* LA CHUNGA's *hand to his chest.*) Here,
feel it now. See how strongly it's beating. As if it were
bursting to get out. That's what happens, whenever I
think of the two of you up there.

(LA CHUNGA's *lips move as if she were saying something.* JOSE
leans over in an attempt to hear what it is, but regrets it
immediately and draws back. For a few moments LA CHUNGA
carries on mouthing the same words in silence. When she
finally articulates, her voice is strangely subdued.)

LA CHUNGA: You're a wanker, José.

JOSE: (*Anxiously, impatiently, pointing towards the little room*)
Please, please, tell me, Chunguita. What happened? What
was it like?

LA CHUNGA: (*Lecturing him, but not severely – as if to a naughty*
child) It's not real women you like, José. Not women of
flesh and blood, at least. The ones you really like are the
ones you keep up here, in your mind – (*Touching his head*
as if caressing it) – but they're only memories, fantasies,
ghosts from the past that live in your imagination, they
don't really exist. Am I right, José?

JOSE: (*Trying to make* LA CHUNGA *get up out of her rocking chair;*
getting more and more excited) You took her by the arm,
and you started to lead her over there. Slowly you began
to climb the staircase, and you never let go of her arm
for a single moment. Did you squeeze it? Did you fondle
it?

(LA CHUNGA *gets up and* JOSE *takes her place in the rocking*
chair. He tilts it – so that he can see better. LA CHUNGA

pours a glass of vermouth, goes up the staircase and into the
little room which is now lit with a reddish light. MECHE *is*
there.)

The voyeur's dream

MECHE: (*With a nervous little laugh*) So now what happens?
What's the game, Chunga?
(*The cold woman of the previous scenes suddenly seems charged*
with life and sensuality.)

LA CHUNGA: It's not a game. I've paid three thousand sols for
you. You're mine for the rest of the night.

MECHE: (*Defiantly*) Do you mean I'm your slave?

LA CHUNGA: For a few hours, at least. (*Handing her the glass*)
Here. It'll calm your nerves.
(MECHE *grasps the glass and takes a gulp.*)

MECHE: Do you think I'm nervous? Well, you're wrong. I'm
not afraid of you. I'm doing this for Josefino. If I wanted
to, I could push you aside and run out that door.
(LA CHUNGA *sits on the bed.*)

LA CHUNGA: But you won't. You said you'd obey me, and
you're a woman of your word, I'm sure. Besides, you're
just dying of curiosity, aren't you?

MECHE: (*Finishing the glass*) Do you honestly think you're going
to get me drunk on two vermouths? Don't kid yourself.
I've got a strong head for drink. I can go on all night
without getting in the least bit tipsy. I can hold even more
than Josefino.
(*Pause.*)

LA CHUNGA: Do to me what you do to him when you want to
excite him.

MECHE: (*With the same nervous little laugh*) I can't. You're a
woman. You're Chunga.

LA CHUNGA: (*Coaxing and at the same time peremptory*) No. I
am Josefino. Do to me what you do to him.
(*Soft tropical music – boleros by Leo Marini or Los Panchos*
– can be heard in the distance. It conjures up images of couples
dancing close, in a place full of smoke and alcohol. MECHE

starts to undress, slowly, and rather awkwardly. Her voice seems forced, and unrelaxed.)

MECHE: You want to see me undress? Slowly, like this? This is how he likes it. Do you think I'm pretty? Do you like my legs? My breasts? I've got a nice firm body, look. No moles, no pimples, no flab. None of those things that make people so ugly.

(*She has stripped down to her petticoat. She feels a little faint. She screws up her face.*)

I can't, Chunga. You're not him. I can't believe what I'm doing or what I'm saying. I feel stupid, all this seems so unreal to me, so. . . .

(*She lets herself fall on the bed and stays there, face down, in a state of confusion; she is on the point of tears, but manages to restrain herself. LA CHUNGA gets up and sits beside her. She acts now with great sensitivity, as if moved by MECHE's discomfort.*)

LA CHUNGA: The truth is, I admire you for being here. You surprised me, you know? I didn't think you would accept. (*Smoothes MECHE's hair.*) Do you love Josefino that much?

MECHE: (*Her voice a whisper*) Yes, I love him. (*Pause.*) But I don't think I did it just for him. But because of what you said too. I was curious. (*Turns to look at LA CHUNGA.*) You gave him three thousand *sols*. That's a lot of money.

LA CHUNGA: (*Passing her hand over MECHE's face, drying non-existent tears*) You're worth more than that.

(*A hint of flirtatiousness becomes apparent through MECHE's resentment and embarrassment.*)

MECHE: Do you really like me, Chunga?

LA CHUNGA: You know very well I do. Or perhaps you didn't realize?

MECHE: Yes, I did. No other woman has ever looked at me like you did. You made me feel . . . so strange.

(*LA CHUNGA puts her hand round MECHE's shoulders and draws her to her. Kisses her. MECHE passively allows herself to be kissed. When they separate MECHE gives a false little laugh.*)

LA CHUNGA: You're laughing – so it can't have been that dreadful.

MECHE: How long have you been like this? I mean, have you always been . . . ? Have you always liked women?

LA CHUNGA: I don't like *women*. I like you.

(*She embraces her and kisses her.* MECHE *lets herself be kissed, but does not respond to* LA CHUNGA's *caresses.* LA CHUNGA *gently draws her face round and, still caressing her, orders her.*) Open your mouth, slave.

(MECHE *giggles nervously, and parts her lips.* LA CHUNGA *gives her a long kiss and this time* MECHE *raises her arm and puts it around* LA CHUNGA's *neck.*)

That's it. I thought you didn't know how to kiss. (*Sarcastically*) Did you see little stars?

MECHE: (*Laughing*) Don't make fun of me.

LA CHUNGA: (*Holding her in her arms*) I'm not making fun of you. I want you to enjoy yourself tonight – more than you've ever enjoyed anything with that pimp.

MECHE: He's not a pimp! Don't say that word. He's in love with me. We may be getting married.

LA CHUNGA: He's a pimp. He sold you to me tonight. Next, he'll be taking you to the Casa Verde, to whore for him like all his other women.

(MECHE *tries to slip away from her arms, pretending to be more angry than she really feels, but after a short struggle, she relents.* LA CHUNGA *puts her face close to hers and talks to her, almost kissing her.*)

Let's not talk about that bum any more. Let's just talk about you and me.

MECHE: (*More calmly*) Don't hold me so tight, you're hurting.

LA CHUNGA: I can do what I want with you. You're my slave.

(MECHE *laughs.*)

Don't laugh. Repeat: I am your slave.

(*Pause.*)

MECHE: (*Laughs. Becoming serious*) It's only a game, isn't it? All right. I am your slave.

LA CHUNGA: I'm your slave and now I want to be your whore. (*Pause.*) Repeat.

MECHE: (*Almost in a whisper*) I'm your slave and now I want to be your whore.

(LA CHUNGA *lays* MECHE *on the bed and starts to undress her.*)

LA CHUNGA: So you will be.

(*The room becomes dark and disappears from view. From the rocking chair,* JOSE *keeps on gazing, mesmerized, into the darkness. At the table where the superstuds are playing dice, the noise starts up again: the noise of toasts being drunk, songs being sung and swearing.*)

Speculations about Meche

The following dialogue takes place as the superstuds carry on playing dice and drinking beer.

LITUMA: Do you want to know something? I sometimes think all this about Mechita disappearing is just another of Josefino's little stories.

EL MONO: Then maybe you'd like to explain it to me – loud and clear – because I don't know what you're talking about.

LITUMA: A woman can't just vanish into thin air, overnight. After all, Piura's only the size of a pocket handkerchief.

JOSEFINO: If she'd stayed in Piura, I'd have found her. No, she scarpered, all right. Maybe to Ecuador. Or Lima. (*Pointing to the rocking chair where* JOSE *is sitting*) She knows, but she'd die rather than give away her little secret, wouldn't you, Chunguita? I lost a woman all because of you, a woman who'd have made me rich, but I don't hold it against you, because basically I've got a heart of gold. Wouldn't you agree?

EL MONO: Don't start up about Mechita again, or you'll give José a hard-on. (*Nudging the invisible* JOSE) It drives you crazy, doesn't it – thinking about them up there, playing with each other?

LITUMA: (*Carrying on, unperturbed*) Someone would have seen her take the bus or a taxi. She would have said goodbye to somebody. She would have packed her things, taken them out of the house. But she left all her clothes and her suitcase behind. No one saw her go. So we can't be so

sure about her running away. Do you know what I
sometimes think, Josefino?

EL MONO: (*Touching* LITUMA's *head*) So you actually think! I
thought donkeys only brayed, ha ha.

JOSEFINO: Well. What *do* you think, Einstein?

LITUMA: You beat her up, didn't you? Don't you beat up every
woman who falls for you? Sometimes I think you go a bit
too far.

JOSEFINO: (*Laughing*) So I killed her? Is that what you're trying
to say? What a profound idea, Lituma.

EL MONO: But this poor bastard couldn't even kill a fly. He's
all mouth, just look at him there poncing around with his
knife in his hand, as if he were the king pimp. I could
knock him over with a feather. Do you want to see?
(*Blows.*) Go on, over you go, don't make a fool of me in
front of my friends.

LITUMA: (*Very seriously, developing his idea*) You could have
been jealous about Mechita spending the night with
Chunga. And you'd just lost everything, down to your
shirt, remember. So you were in a really filthy temper.
You went home like a wild beast on the rampage. You
needed to take it out on someone. Meche was there, and
she was the one who got it in the neck. You could easily
have gone too far.

JOSEFINO: (*Amused*) And then I cut her up into little pieces and
threw her in the river? Is that it? You're a bloody genius
Lituma. (*To the absent* JOSE, *handing him the dice*) Here,
José, it's your turn to win now. The dice are all yours.

LITUMA: Poor Meche. She didn't deserve a son of a bitch like
you, Josefino.

JOSEFINO: The things one has to put up with from one's friends.
If you weren't a superstud, I'd cut your balls off and
throw them to the dogs.

EL MONO: Do you want to poison the poor little brutes? What
harm have they ever done to you, for Christ's sake?
(JOSE *goes back to his seat, as discreetly as he left it. At the
same time, without the other three being aware of him,*
LITUMA *gets up and leaves the table.*)

JOSEFINO: (*To* JOSE) Why are you so quiet? What's up, mate?

JOSE: I'm losing and I don't feel like talking. That's all. Right, now my luck is going to change. (*Picks up the dice and blows on them. Puts a banknote on the table.*) There's a hundred little *sols*. Who's going to take me on? (*Addressing Lituma's chair as if he were still there*) You, Lituma? (*In the two following scenes,* JOSE, EL MONO *and* JOSEFINO *behave as if* LITUMA *were still with them. But* LITUMA *is now at the foot of the small flight of stairs watching* LA CHUNGA's *little room, which has just been lit up.*)

Pimping

LA CHUNGA *and* MECHE *are dressed. There is no sign whatever of them having undressed or made love. Their outward behaviour is very different from the previous scene in which they appeared.* MECHE *is sitting on the bed, a little dejected, and* LA CHUNGA, *who is standing in front of the bed, doesn't seem at all like the sensual or domineering woman she was before, but rather more enigmatic and machiavellian.* MECHE *lights a cigarette. Draws the smoke into her lungs, trying to hide the fact that she feels uneasy.*

MECHE: If you think he's ever going to give you back those three thousand *sols*, you must be dreaming.

LA CHUNGA: I know I'll never get them back. I don't mind.

MECHE: (*Scrutinizing her, intrigued*) Do you really expect me to believe you, Chunga? Do you think I don't know you're the most tight-fisted woman in town, that you work day and night like a black so you can keep on coining it in?

LA CHUNGA: I mean, *in this case*, I don't mind. Just as well for you, isn't it? If I hadn't given him that money, Josefino would have taken it all out on you.

MECHE: Yes. He would've beaten me up. Every time something goes wrong, every time he's in a bad mood, I'm the one who pays for it. (*Pause.*) One of these days, he's going to kill me.

LA CHUNGA: Why do you stay with him, silly?

MECHE: I don't know . . . maybe that's why. Because I'm silly.

LA CHUNGA: He beats you up and you still love him?

MECHE: I don't really know if I love him. I did to begin with. Now maybe I stay with him just because I'm scared, Chunga. He's . . . a brute. Sometimes even if I've done nothing, he makes me kneel down before him, as if he were a god. He takes out his knife and draws it across here. 'Be grateful you're still alive,' he says. 'You're living on borrowed time, don't ever forget that.'

LA CHUNGA: And you still stay with him? How stupid women can be. I'll never understand how anyone can sink so low.

MECHE: You've obviously never been in love.

LA CHUNGA: And I never will be. I prefer to live without a man. In total solitude. No one's ever going to make me go down on my knees. Or tell me I'm living on borrowed time.

MECHE: Ah, if only I could break loose from Josefino . . .

LA CHUNGA: (*Like a spider attracting a fly into the web she's spun for it*) But you can, silly. (*Smiling mischievously*) Have you forgotten how pretty you are? Don't you realize what you do to men when you walk past? None of them can take their eyes off you. Don't they pay you all sorts of compliments? Don't they make you propositions when he's out of earshot?

MECHE: Yes. I could have been unfaithful to him a thousand times, if I'd wanted to. I've had plenty of chances.

LA CHUNGA: (*Sitting beside her*) Of course you have. But perhaps you haven't realized the best chance you ever had.

MECHE: (*Surprised*) Who are you talking about?

LA CHUNGA: Someone who's crazy about you. Someone who'd do anything you asked, just to be with you, because he thinks you're the most beautiful, the most exquisite creature alive – a queen, a goddess. You could have him at your feet, Meche. He'd never ill-treat or frighten you.

MECHE: But who are you talking about?

LA CHUNGA: Haven't you noticed? I suppose it's understandable. He's very shy with women . . .

MECHE: Now I know why you gave those three thousand *sols*

193

to Josefino. Not because you're a dike. But because you're
a pimp, Chunga.

LA CHUNGA: (*Laughing, warmly and affectionately*) Did you
think I was going to pay three thousand *sols* to make love
to you? No, Mechita, no man or woman alive is worth that
much to me. Those three thousand *sols* aren't mine. They
belong to the man who loves you. He's prepared to spend
all he's got and more just to have you. Be nice to him.
Remember you promised to do whatever I asked. Now's
your chance to get your own back on Josefino for all those
thrashings. Make the most of it.
(LITUMA *has gone up the little staircase and is at the door of
the room, but he doesn't dare go in.* LA CHUNGA *goes out to
meet him.*)
Go on in. She's there waiting for you. She's yours. I've
already had a word with her, don't worry. Go on, Lituma,
don't be frightened. She's all yours, enjoy it.
(*With a sardonic little laugh, she leaves the room and goes to
sit down in her rocking chair. The superstuds carry on drinking
and gambling.*)

A romantic love affair

MECHE: (*Surprised*) So it was you. The last person I would have
suspected. Mono or José, perhaps – they're always flirting
with me, and they sometimes go even further when Josefino
isn't looking. But you, Lituma, you've never said a single
word to me.

LITUMA: (*Deeply embarrassed*) I've never dared, Mechita. I've
never quite been able to show what I felt about you. But,
but I . . .

MECHE: (*Amused at his awkwardness*) You're all sweaty, your
voice is trembling, you're so shy, it's painful. How funny
you are, Lituma.

LITUMA: (*Imploring*) Please, don't laugh at me, Meche. For the
love of God . . . I beg you . . .

MECHE: Have you always been frightened of women?

LITUMA: (*Very sorrowfully*) Not frightened exactly. It's just that . . . I never know what to say to them. I'm not like the others. When they meet a girl they know how to chat her up, and make a date with her. I've never been able to do that. I get so worked up, I can't get the words out.

MECHE: Haven't you ever had a girlfriend?

LITUMA: I've never had a woman without paying for her, Mechita. Only the whores at the Casa Verde. And they always make me pay.

MECHE: Just like you're paying for me now.

LITUMA: (*Kneeling before* MECHE) Don't compare yourself with those whores, Mechita, not even in fun.

MECHE: What are you doing?

LITUMA: I'd never make you go down on your knees to me, like Josefino does. I'd spend my life on my knees in front of you. I'd worship you, Meche, as if you were a queen. (*He crouches down and tries to kiss her feet.*)

MECHE: Ha ha, when you do that, you're just like a little lapdog.

LITUMA: (*Still trying to kiss her feet*) Then at least let me be your lapdog, Meche. I'll obey you, I'll be loving and gentle whenever you want or if you'd rather I'll just lie still. Don't laugh, I'm being serious.

MECHE: Would you really do anything for me?

LITUMA: Try me.

MECHE: Would you kill Josefino if I asked you to?

LITUMA: Yes.

MECHE: But I thought he was your friend.

LITUMA: You're worth more to me than any friend, Mechita. Do you believe that?

(MECHE *puts her hand on his head, as if stroking an animal.*)

MECHE: Come, and sit beside me. I don't want anyone to grovel to me like that.

LITUMA: (*Sitting beside her, on the bed, without daring to go very close to her or even touch her*) I've been in love with you since the first day I saw you. In the Río-Bar, on the Old Bridge. Don't you remember? No. Why should you remember? You never seemed to take any notice of me, even when you were looking straight at me.

MECHE: In the Río-Bar?

LITUMA: José, Mono and I were in the middle of a game, when in came Josefino with you on his arm. (*Imitating him*) Hey, look what I've found. What d'you think of her, eh? Then he lifted you up by the waist and paraded you in front of everyone. (*His face suddenly clouds over.*) I hate him when he does things like that to you.

MECHE: Does he make you jealous?

LITUMA: No, he makes me envious, though. (*Pause.*) Tell me, Mechita. Is it true he's got one this big? Is that why women are so crazy about him? He never stops bragging to us: 'Mine's a real whopper,' he says. But I've asked the whores in the Casa Verde and they say it's not true, that it's the normal size – just like everyone else's.

MECHE: You aren't going to have much success with me if you say such disgusting things, Lituma.

LITUMA: I'm sorry. You're right, I shouldn't have asked you that. But, doesn't it seem unfair? Josefino behaves so boorishly with women. He knocks them around, they fall in love with him, and when he's got them really hooked, he sends them out to whore for him. And in spite of that, he still gets the ones he wants. Yet someone like me, who's an honest, well-meaning, gentlemanly sort, who'd be prepared to treat any woman who loved him like precious china, never gets any attention at all. I ask you, is that fair?

MECHE: It may not be fair. But is anything in life fair?

LITUMA: Is it because I'm ugly that they don't pay any attention to me, Mechita?

MECHE: (*Making fun of him*) Here. Let me have a look at you. No, you're not that ugly, Lituma.

LITUMA: Please be serious with me. I'm telling you things I've never told anyone in my life before.

(MECHE *looks at him for a moment mistrustfully.*)

MECHE: Did you fall in love with me the first time you saw me?

LITUMA: (*nodding*) I didn't sleep all night. In the darkness, I kept seeing you. I thought you were the most beautiful woman I'd ever seen. I thought women like you only

existed in the cinema. I worked myself up into such a
state that I even cried, Mechita. I can't tell you how many
nights I've lain awake, thinking about you.

MECHE: And you say you don't know how to talk to women.
It's beautiful, what you're telling me.

(LITUMA *puts his hand in his pocket and takes out a small
photograph.*)

LITUMA: Look. I always carry you around with me.

MECHE: Where did you get that photo from?

LITUMA: I stole it from Josefino. It's a bit faded – with all the
kissing I've given it.

MECHE: (*Stroking his head again*) Why didn't you ever say
anything to me before, silly?

LITUMA: We've still time, haven't we? Marry me, Mechita.
Let's leave Piura. Let's start a new life.

MECHE: But you're broke, Lituma. Like the rest of the
superstuds. And you've never done a day's work in your
life, either.

LITUMA: Because I've never had anyone to push me, to make
me change the way I live. You don't think I enjoy being
a superstud, do you? Marry me – you'll see how different
I can be, Mechita. I'll work hard, I'll do anything. You'll
always have everything you want.

MECHE: Would we go to Lima?

LITUMA: To Lima, yes. Or wherever you want.

MECHE: I've always wanted to go to Lima. It's such a large
city, Josefino would never find us.

LITUMA: Of course not. And besides what would it matter if
he did find us? Are you afraid of him?

MECHE: Yes.

LITUMA: With me you wouldn't be. He's quite harmless, really,
he's just a loud mouth. I know him very well – we were
kids together. He's not from round here, of course – he's
from the Gallinacera. There, they're all talk and no action.

MECHE: Well, he's not all talk with me. He sometimes beats
me practically unconscious. If I left him to go away with
you, he'd kill me.

LITUMA: Nonsense, Meche. He'd get himself another woman, just like that. Let's go to Lima. Tonight.

MECHE: (*Tempted*) Tonight?

LITUMA: We'll catch the bus from the Cruz de Chalpón. Come on.

MECHE: Shall we get married?

LITUMA: As soon as we get to Lima, I promise you. It's the first thing we'll do. Would you like that? Shall we go? (*Pause.*)

MECHE: Let's go. We'll never return to Piura. I hope I won't live to regret this one day, Lituma.

LITUMA: (*Kneeling again*) I promise you never will, Mechita. Thank you, thank you. Ask me for something, anything you want, just tell me to do something.

MECHE: Get up, we've no time to waste. Go and pack your suitcase, and buy the tickets. Wait for me at the Cruz de Chalpón bus station. Halfway up Avenida Grau, all right? I'll be there, just before twelve.

LITUMA: Where are you going?

MECHE: I can't just leave without taking anything with me. I'm going to fetch my things. Just a few essentials.

LITUMA: I'll come with you.

MECHE: No, it's not necessary. Josefino is in the Casa Verde and he never gets back till dawn – I've got more than enough time. We mustn't be seen together on the street though, no one must suspect a thing.

LITUMA: (*Kissing her hands*) Mechita, Mechita, darling. I'm so happy I can't believe it's true. (*Crosses himself, looks at the sky.*) Thank you God, dear sweet God. From now on I'm going to be different, I'm going to stop being lazy – I'm going to stop gambling, living it up, lying . . . I swear to you . . .

MECHE: (*Pushing him*) Come on, hurry up, we're wasting time, Lituma. Quickly, run . . .

LITUMA: Yes, yes, whatever you say, Mechita.

(*He gets up hurriedly, rushes towards the staircase, but there he loses his impetus. He slows down – comes to a halt – and slowly returns to the gambling table, weary and sad. The*

198

superstuds do not notice him. Once again the central focus is on them, as they continue to gamble, swear and drink toasts to each other.)

Fantasies on a crime

EL MONO: And why not? Lituma's right, it could have happened like that. Just shut your eyes for a moment and imagine Mechita: she rushes into the house looking frantically around to left and right, her little buttocks all clenched with fear.

JOSE: She starts to throw things into her suitcase at breakneck speed, trembling all over, tripping over the furniture, packing the wrong things, unpacking them again, panic-stricken at the thought that at any moment who might arrive but the Great Pimp himself. Out of sheer anxiety her little nipples have become as hard as pebbles. Scrumptious.

JOSEFINO: (*Laughing*) And then what? Go on. What happened next?

LITUMA: Then you arrived. Before she finished packing.

JOSEFINO: And I killed her because I caught her packing her suitcase?

EL MONO: No. That would have been your excuse. You killed her because you were furious at the way things had turned out. Remember, I'd practically taken the shirt off your back. Shit, if I ever have another hand like the one I had that night. Holy Whore!

JOSE: Or maybe you got an attack of jealousy. Perhaps Meche told you that Chunga had made her so happy that she was going to come and live with her.

JOSEFINO: I wouldn't have killed her for that. I'd probably have sent Chunga some flowers. And a postcard saying: 'Congratulations. You won.' I'm a bloody fine sport you know!

LA CHUNGA: (*From her armchair, yawning*) It's nearly twelve and I'm tired. Last orders.

LITUMA: Quiet, Chunga, you're ruining my inspiration. When

you saw she was in the middle of packing, you asked her,
'Off for a little holiday then, are we?' 'I'm leaving you,'
she said.

JOSEFINO: And why would she leave me? She was completely
besotted with me.

LITUMA: (*Serious and self-absorbed, not hearing him*) 'I'm leaving
you because I'm in love with a better man than you.'

JOSEFINO: Better than me? And where did she dig up this . . .
paragon?

LITUMA: 'Someone who won't beat me, someone who'll be
faithful to me, and be good to me. Someone who's not a
bastard or a pimp, but who's decent and honest. And,
what's more, who's prepared to marry me.'

JOSEFINO: What a fantastic load of crap. None of you lot can
find a single good reason why I should have killed
Mechita.

LITUMA: You were beside yourself with rage, Josefino. So you
laid into her savagely. You probably only intended to give
her a trouncing. But you got carried away and finished the
poor little thing off.

JOSEFINO: I see. And what the hell did I do with the body?

EL MONO: You threw it in the river.

JOSEFINO: It was September. The river is dry in September.
What did I do with the body? Come on, guess. Tell me
how I committed my perfect crime?

JOSE: You buried it in the sand, behind your house.

EL MONO: You threw it to the dogs – those German beasts that
guard Señor Beckman's warehouse. They wouldn't even
leave the small bones.

JOSE: OK, I'm bored with these detective games. Let's go down
to the Casa Verde for a quick one. Coming?

JOSEFINO: Why go so far, when you've got Chunga there? Go
on, give her a taste of what she likes.

LA CHUNGA: I'll tell him who he can give 'a taste of what she
likes' to, Josefino, you bastard.

JOSEFINO: Are you insulting my mother by any chance,
Chunga? Now that's one thing I won't stand for.

LA CHUNGA: Then don't you insult me.

EL MONO: Take no notice of him, Chunguita. You've got to
make allowances. He's from the Gallinacera, remember.

JOSE: It's a pity you're always so bad-tempered, Chunga.
Specially with us, who are so fond of you. You know
you're our lucky mascot.

(EL MONO *gets up without his friends noticing and approaches*
LA CHUNGA.)

EL MONO: These tykes are always getting under your skin,
aren't they, Chunga? You've got to forgive them – they're
just a bunch of ignoramuses. But I always behave myself,
don't I? I hope you've noticed that. I don't upset you, or
make fun of you – and I don't join in when they're annoying
you either. I love you very much, Chunga.

LA CHUNGA: (*Looking at him compassionately*) You don't have
to put on that good-little-boy act with me. What's the
point? I'm going to give you a good time, whatever you
do. Come, give me your hand.

(*She takes his hand and leads him to the staircase. She goes
up with him. He looks happy; his eyes have lit up, like a
child who's about to satisfy a burning ambition. The superstuds
carry on gambling with El Mono's ghost.*)

A naughty little boy

MECHE: Hello, Monito.

EL MONO: Hello, Meche.

LA CHUNGA: Come in, don't be afraid, we're not going to hurt
you.

EL MONO: I know you're both very kind.

MECHE: Come and sit down here, beside me.

(EL MONO *sits on the bed, next to* MECHE. LA CHUNGA *sits
on the other side. The two women treat* EL MONO *as if he
were a spoilt child, and he too, in his expression and behaviour,
seems to have regressed to childhood. A sigh escapes him. And
another. It would appear something is preying on his mind,
something he would like to share with them, but doesn't dare.*)

LA CHUNGA: Relax, make yourself at home. Now what's on

your mind? Don't be shy, you're the boss. Your wish is our
command.

MECHE: We're here to please you in whatever way we can.
Now, what turns you on?

LA CHUNGA: Do you want us to do a striptease for you, Monito?

MECHE: Want us to dance together naked, just for you?

EL MONO: (*Hiding his face in horror*) No. No. Please.

LA CHUNGA: (*Pointing at the bed*) Would you like us to go to
bed together, the three of us, with you in the middle?

MECHE: Like us to stroke you, until you shout, 'Stop, stop, I
can't stand any more?'

LA CHUNGA: Do you want us to pose for you?

EL MONO: (*Laughing, very nervously*) Don't joke like that,
please, it embarrasses me. (*Overcome by a sudden attack
of melancholy*) You're such good people, Chunga, Mechita.
I'm sorry I'm behaving like this, but I'm not like you. I . . .
I'm a shit.

LA CHUNGA: Don't say that. It's not true.

MECHE: A bit of a clown, perhaps. But you're a good boy really,
Monito.

EL MONO: You're wrong. I'm not good at all. I'm one of the
worst, filthiest little boys around. And don't try and tell
me I'm not. You see, the trouble is, neither of you really
knows. If I were to tell you . . .

LA CHUNGA: Come on then, tell us.

MECHE: You want us to comfort you? Is that what you want?

EL MONO: I don't want to force you into anything. Only if you
insist . . .

(LA CHUNGA *makes him rest his head on her lap.* EL MONO
curls up like a frightened child.)

LA CHUNGA: Come on, rest your head here. Make yourself
comfortable.

MECHE: (*In a soft, caressing voice*) Tell us, Monito.

EL MONO: (*Nervously, and with great difficulty*) I didn't even
realize what I was doing. I was very young, a little boy
in short trousers.

LA CHUNGA: Are you talking about what happened with the
little girl next door? Doña Jesusa's daughter.

LA CHUNGA

EL MONO: I was only a little boy. Do little boys act sensibly?

MECHE: Of course not, Monito. So, carry on. I'll help you. You were keeping watch – waiting for Doña Jesusa to go out to the market, to her vegetable stall . . .

LA CHUNGA: And when she came out, you went into her house without anyone seeing you. Jumping over the bamboo fence by the banana plantation. Wasn't that it?

EL MONO: Yes. And there she was, squatting down, milking the goat. She was squeezing its teats. Like this. And she wasn't wearing any knickers, Chunga! I swear it!

MECHE: Don't worry, we believe you. So you saw everything.

EL MONO: Or rather she showed me everything, Mechita. Why else would she be knickerless? Why else would she be? So that people would see her little thing, so that she could show it off to the men.

LA CHUNGA: Do you mean that she provoked you, Monito? Then you're not to blame for anything. She was asking for it, the dirty brazen little hussy.

MECHE: Is that what you wanted to tell us? That it was all her fault?

EL MONO: (Sadly) Well, no. I was a little bit to blame, too. I mean I did sneak secretly into Doña Jesusa's house, didn't I? That's what burglars do, isn't it?

LA CHUNGA: But you didn't go in to steal anything, Monito.

EL MONO: No. I just went in to see the girl.

MECHE: Did you want to see her naked?

EL MONO: I was only small, you understand. I didn't know what I was doing. I couldn't yet tell the difference between right and wrong.

LA CHUNGA: But you had a knife, this long, Mono. Remember?

EL MONO: I remember.

MECHE: Didn't you feel sorry for the girl? Not even when she smiled at you, thinking that it was just an innocent little prank.

EL MONO: It *was* an innocent little prank. But she had no knickers on, Meche. She provoked me. She led me on . . .

LA CHUNGA: (Admonishing him, not very severely) Come on, tell

203

us the truth, Monito. She did have knickers on. You
made her take them off.

MECHE: By threatening to kill her. Yes or no, Monito?

EL MONO: Well, perhaps. It's a long time ago now. I've
forgotten.

LA CHUNGA: Lies. You haven't forgotten. You tore off her
dress and ordered her to take down her knickers. And
when she did, you saw what you wanted to see. Isn't that
it, Monito?

EL MONO: (*Ashamed*) Yes, Chunguita.

MECHE: And you fondled her, didn't you? And you felt her all
over. Yes or no?

EL MONO: (*Distressed*) But I didn't rape her, Meche. I swear to
Almighty God I didn't rape her. Not that.

LA CHUNGA: You didn't rape her? Well, what did you do then?
Doesn't it come to the same thing?

EL MONO: (*Laughing*) How can it be the same thing! Don't be
silly, Chunga. (*Lowering his voice and lifting a finger to his
lips, going* shhht! shhht! *as if he were going to reveal a great
secret*) I put it up her little one, don't you see? But she
remained intact where it counted. There wasn't a blemish,
not even a scratch, it was all in one piece for her husband
to break on the night of his wedding. It's a very important
distinction. Ask Padre García if you like. 'If the hymen
isn't broken, I'll absolve you. But if it is, there's no excuse,
you little so-and-so, you'll have to marry Jesusa's little
girl.' Well, she didn't marry me, in other words . . . You
women keep your honour in that tiny little treasure chest
– that's why you must protect it, tooth and nail. But we
men, on the other hand, keep our honour round the other
side. And woe betide anyone who gets it up his little one,
because bingo, he's buggered for the rest of his life.
(LA CHUNGA *and* MECHE *look at him, teasing and silent –
and he becomes sad and remorseful. He sits up.*)
Yes, it's true, you're right about what you're thinking. It
was very wicked what I did to the little girl. I could fool
Padre García, but not you. I know that when I die, God
will punish me for it.

LA CHUNGA: Why wait so long, Monito?

MECHE: We could punish you now.

(EL MONO *takes off his belt and gives it to her. He adopts a position suitable for being whipped.*)

All right. Take away all my filth – make me pay for my wickedness. Don't spare me. Take away my honour, Chunga, Mechita.

LA CHUNGA and MECHE: (*As they beat him*) Naughty little boy! You bad-mannered child! You beastly little boy! You depraved child! Vicious little boy! Wicked child! Degenerate!

(EL MONO *groans, receives the strokes, cowering, sweating with a sense of enjoyment that culminates in a spasm of ecstacy.* MECHE *and* LA CHUNGA *sit down and watch him. Satisfied but melancholy, he stands up, wipes his forehead, puts on his belt again and combs his hair. Without looking at them he leaves the room discreetly and takes his place again at the table of the superstuds.*)

LA CHUNGA: Are you going without even saying goodbye or thank you, Monito?

MECHE: Come back and tell us more whenever you like, Monito.

Two friends

As soon as EL MONO *disappears from the room,* MECHE *and* LA CHUNGA *change their demeanour, as if the previous scene had not taken place.*

LA CHUNGA: Some are better actors than others. But you only have to scratch a little beneath the surface, and there's a wild beast waiting to pounce.

MECHE: Do you think all men are like that, Chunga? Have they all got something nasty to hide?

LA CHUNGA: All the ones I know do.

MECHE: Are we women any better?

LA CHUNGA: At least what we've got between our legs doesn't turn us into foul demons.

MECHE: (*Touching her stomach*) Then I hope to goodness it's a girl.

LA CHUNGA: Are you pregnant?

MECHE: I haven't had a period for two months.

LA CHUNGA: Haven't you been to see anyone?

MECHE: I'm afraid they'll tell me I am.

LA CHUNGA: Don't you want to have it?

MECHE: Of course I do. But Josefino doesn't. If I'm pregnant, he'll make me get rid of it. No woman's going to tie him down with a child, he says.

LA CHUNGA: He's right there, I grant him. I don't think it's worth while bringing more people into this world. What do you want a child for? If it's a boy, he'll only grow up to be just like one of *them*.

MECHE: If everyone thought like that, life would soon come to an end.

LA CHUNGA: It could end tomorrow for all I care.
(*Pause.*)

MECHE: Do you know something, Chunga? I don't think you're as bitter as you'd have me believe.

LA CHUNGA: And what would I have you believe?

MECHE: If you were, I wouldn't be here. (*There is a twinkle in her eye.*) You wouldn't have given Josefino those three thousand *sols* for me to spend the night with you. Besides . . .

LA CHUNGA: Besides what?

MECHE: (*Indicating the bed*) A little while ago, when you were holding me in your arms, you said some very tender things to me. That I made you feel as if you were in heaven, that you were happy. Were you lying to me?

LA CHUNGA: No. It was true.

MECHE: So life isn't so ugly after all. It has its advantages too. (*Laughs*) I'm glad I'm one of the good things life has to offer you, Chunga. (*Pause.*) Can I ask you a question?

LA CHUNGA: If it's how many women have been here before you, it's better you don't. I'm not going to tell you, anyway.

MECHE: No, it's not that. But, could you ever fall in love with

me, Chunga? Like a man does with a woman? Could you
ever love me?

LA CHUNGA: I wouldn't fall in love with you or with anyone
else.

MECHE: I don't believe you, Chunga. No one can live without
love. What would life be like if you didn't love someone,
if you weren't loved by anyone?

LA CHUNGA: When a woman falls in love, she becomes weak.
She lets herself be dominated. (*Looks at her in silence for
a while.*) Now do you think that's a good thing? We'll talk
about it again when you see what Josefino does with your
love. We'll talk about it when you're in the Casa Verde.

MECHE: Why do you keep frightening me with that?

LA CHUNGA: Because I know what will happen to you. He's
got you in the palm of his hand, he already does what he
likes with you. One of these nights, in a fit of drunkenness,
he'll lend you to one of the superstuds, but that's just the
beginning. He'll end up by persuading you to whore for
him, with some cock and bull story about saving money
for a little house, or a holiday, or to get married.

MECHE: When you tell me these things, I don't know if you're
doing it out of kindness or spite. If you really want to
help me, or if you just like frightening me.

LA CHUNGA: I want to help you.

MECHE: But why? You couldn't be in love with me, could you?
You've just said you weren't. Why should you want to
help me, you, to whom everything is like water off a duck's
back – you who don't give a damn about anyone.

LA CHUNGA: (*Looking at her, thinking*) You're right. I don't
know why I'm giving you advice. Why should your life
matter to me?

MECHE: Have you given advice before to one of Josefino's
girlfriends?

LA CHUNGA: No.
(*She looks closely at* MECHE. *Takes her chin in her hand and
forces her to look her in the eyes. She puts her face very close
to* MECHE's.)
Perhaps I feel sorrier for you than I did for the others,

because you're more attractive. Another one of life's
injustices. If you didn't have such a pretty little face, I'm
quite sure I wouldn't give a damn what Josefino did with
you.

MECHE: Sometimes I think you're a monster, Chunga.

LA CHUNGA: Because you don't want to see life as it is. It's life
that's monstrous. Not me.

MECHE: If life is as you say it is, it's preferable to be like me.
And not to think about what's going to happen. Just live
for the moment. And let God take care of the rest.
(*She looks at her stomach, with an expression of despair.*)

LA CHUNGA: Perhaps you'll work that miracle: perhaps you'll
reform Josefino.

MECHE: You know that won't happen.

LA CHUNGA: No. It won't happen.
(MECHE *leans against* LA CHUNGA *and rests her head on her
shoulder.* LA CHUNGA *doesn't embrace her.*)

MECHE: I wish I was strong like you. You know your own
worth, you can stick up for yourself. If I didn't have anyone
to look after me, I don't know what I'd do.

LA CHUNGA: You've got two hands, haven't you?

MECHE: I can hardly read, Chunga. Where would I find work?
Except as a servant. Sweeping, washing, ironing,
morning, noon and night for the rich men of Piura. No, I
wouldn't do that.
(*Pause.*)

LA CHUNGA: If I'd known that you might be pregnant, I
wouldn't have made love to you.

MECHE: Do pregnant women disgust you?

LA CHUNGA: Yes. (*Pause.*) Did it upset you, what we did?

MECHE: Upset me? I don't know. I don't . . .

LA CHUNGA: Tell me the truth.

MECHE: At first, yes, a bit. I felt like laughing. I mean, you're
not a man, are you? It didn't seem real, it was like a
game. I was trying not to laugh, at first.

LA CHUNGA: If you had laughed . . .

MECHE: You'd have hit me?

LA CHUNGA: Yes, I'd probably have hit you.

MECHE: And yet you were saying that it was only men who are turned into foul demons by what they have between their legs.

LA CHUNGA: I must be a man, then.

MECHE: No, you're not. You're a woman. You could be an attractive woman too, if you wanted to be.

LA CHUNGA: I don't want to be attractive. No one would respect me if I were.

MECHE: Did what I said annoy you?

LA CHUNGA: About trying not to laugh? No, I asked you to tell me the truth.

MECHE: I want you to know something, Chunga. Although I'm not a dike, sorry – like you, I mean – I am fond of you. I'd like us to be friends.

LA CHUNGA: Go on, leave Piura. Don't be silly. Can't you see you're already half caught in the trap? Before Josefino gives you the *coup de grâce*, get out of here. As far away as you can. You've still got time. (*Turns* MECHE's *face towards her with her hand.*) I'll help you.

MECHE: Will you really, Chunga?

LA CHUNGA: Yes. (*Strokes* MECHE's *face with her hand again in a swift caress.*) I don't want to see you rotting away in the Casa Verde, being passed around from one drunk to another . . . Go on, take my advice and go to Lima.

MECHE: What'll I do in Lima? I don't know anyone there.

LA CHUNGA: Learn how to stand on your own feet. But don't be stupid. Don't go and fall in love. It distracts you and there's no hope for a distracted woman. Let *them* do the falling in love. Not you. You look for security, a better life than the one you have now. But always remember this. Deep down, all men are like Josefino. If you show too much affection for them, you've had it.

MECHE: Don't talk like that, Chunga. You know when you say things like that, you remind me of him?

LA CHUNGA: Then Josefino and I must have something in common.

(*As if the mention of his name had been a summons,* JOSEFINO

*gets up from the superstuds' table and goes up the little
staircase.*)

The great pimp

Although MECHE *is in the little room and follows with interest what
is being said,* JOSEFINO *and* LA CHUNGA *act as if she is not
there.*

JOSEFINO: Hello, Chunga. (*Looks round and casts his eyes over*
MECHE *without seeing her.*) I've come to take Meche away
with me.
LA CHUNGA: She's gone already.
JOSEFINO: So soon? You could have held on to her a little bit
longer. (*With an impudent little laugh*) Then you could
really have got your money's worth.
(LA CHUNGA *confines herself to looking at him with that
expression of reproof and disgust with which she always looks
at him.*)
Well, how was she? What was it like?
LA CHUNGA: What was what like?
JOSEFINO: Mechita. Was she worth it?
LA CHUNGA: You've been on the booze all night, haven't you?
You stink from head to foot.
JOSEFINO: What else could I do, Chunguita, since you'd taken
away my little woman. So, tell me, how did Meche
behave?
LA CHUNGA: I'm not going to tell you. It wasn't in the contract.
JOSEFINO: (*Laughing*) You're right. Ha ha. Next time I'll put
in a special clause. (*Pause.*) Why don't you like me,
Chunga? Don't lie, I realize that you've never seen eye to
eye with me.
LA CHUNGA: I've no reason to lie. You're quite right. I've
always thought you were one of the most poisonous
creatures alive.
JOSEFINO: And yet I've always had a soft spot for you. Quite
seriously, Chunga.
LA CHUNGA: (*Laughing*) Are you going to try and seduce me

too? Go on. Show me how you lure all those poor idiots into your snare.

JOSEFINO: No, I'm not going to try and seduce you. (*Undressing her with his look*) It's not because I don't want to, I assure you. Actually, I find you quite attractive as a woman. But I know when I'm defeated. I'd be wasting my time with you, you wouldn't take any notice of me. And I've never wasted time with women.

LA CHUNGA: Right then, be off with you.

JOSEFINO: First, let's talk. I want to make you a proposition. A deal.

LA CHUNGA: A deal? Between you and me?
(JOSEFINO *sits on the bed, lights a cigarette. It's clear that he's thought about what he's going to say for a long time.*)

JOSEFINO: I don't want to carry on being what I am, Chunga. A superstud and all that. Hell, I've got ambitions. I want to have money, drink champagne, smoke expensive tobacco, wear white silk suits, have my own car, my own house, servants. I want to be able to travel. I want to live like the rich do round here, Chunga. That's what you want too, isn't it? That's why you work, morning, noon and night, that's what you practically sell your soul for. Because you want another life, one you can only get with money. Let's become partners, Chunga. You and I together, we could do great things.

LA CHUNGA: I know what you're going to propose.

JOSEFINO: All the better, then.

LA CHUNGA: The answer is no.

JOSEFINO: Why are you so prejudiced? What's the difference between this little bar and a brothel? I'll tell you what: here you earn a few miserable cents, but in a brothel you'd make millions. (*Standing up, gesticulating, walking round the room*) I've got everything taped, Chunga. We can start with about four little rooms. They can be built round the back, behind the kitchen, in the yard where the rubbish is dumped. Nothing fancy, just straw matting and bamboo. I'll take charge of the girls. All first class guaranteed. In the Casa Verde they take 50 per cent off them. We'll take

forty so we'll be able to pull whichever ones we want. Just
a few at first – quality rather than quantity. I'll see to the
discipline and you can do the administration. (*Anxiously,
vehemently*) We'll become rich, Chunguita.

LA CHUNGA: If I'd wanted to set up a brothel, I'd have done
it already. What do I need you for?

JOSEFINO: For the girls. I may be all sorts of things. But in
that particular field, have I proved my worth or not? I'm
the best there is, Chunga. I'll get first-rate girls – ones that
haven't worked before. Virgins even, you'll see. Young
fifteen-, sixteen-year-olds. The clients will go out of their
minds, Chunga. We'll have all the little rich boys in Piura,
prepared to pay the earth – for fresh young girls, who are
just starting out in the world . . .

LA CHUNGA: Like Meche?

JOSEFINO: Well, Meche is not so fresh any more, ha ha . . .
We'd keep her as the resident celebrity, the star
attraction, of course. I swear to you I'll get girls as good
if not better than Meche, Chunga.

LA CHUNGA: And what if they don't want to work?

JOSEFINO: That's my affair. I may not know much else, but
teaching a girl that what God gave her is a prize lottery
ticket, that I do know how to do. Because of me fortunes
have been made at the Casa Verde. And what do I get in
return? Bloody hell, a few mangy tips. Well I've had
enough of it, now I want to be a capitalist too. What do
you say, Chunguita?

LA CHUNGA: I've already told you. No.

JOSEFINO: Why, Chunga? Don't you trust me?

LA CHUNGA: Of course I don't trust you. The very day after
we went into partnership, you'd start lying to me and
cheating me.

JOSEFINO: I wouldn't, Chunga. I promise you. You'd handle
all the money. I'd be prepared to accept that. You'd be
responsible for the agreements with the girls, you'd decide
on the percentages. I wouldn't touch a cent. You'd have
carte blanche. We'd do what you decide. What more do
you want? Don't look a gift horse in the mouth.

LA CHUNGA: You'll never be anyone's gift horse, Josefino. And
certainly not a woman's. You're bad luck for any poor
woman who's gullible enough to believe what you say.

JOSEFINO: So you've become all righteous now, Chunguita?
I've never pointed a pistol at any woman's head. I just
convince them of one truth. That in one night at the Casa
Verde they can earn more money than working for six
months in the market. Well, am I right, or not? Thanks
to me, some of those women live better than we do, for
God's sake.

LA CHUNGA: It's not because I'm righteous that I don't want
to be your partner. I don't feel sorry for them. If they
were stupid enough to listen to you, they deserve whatever
they get.

JOSEFINO: I don't like the way you're talking to me, Chunga.
I came here peacefully, to make you a sound proposition.
And you insult me. What if I do get annoyed? Do you
think a dike like you is any match for me? (*As he speaks
he gets more and more irritated.*) Do you know what could
happen if I got annoyed? The truth is I'm fed up with these
airs and graces you give yourself, as if you own the whole
fucking world. I've had enough of it, Christ Almighty.
I'm going to teach you a lesson, and put you in your place.
You've been asking for it now for quite some time. No
woman, let alone a dike, is going to look down on me.
(*He takes out his knife and threatens* LA CHUNGA, *as if she
were still in front of him. But in fact,* LA CHUNGA *has discreetly
moved beside* MECHE. *Both look at* JOSEFINO *who carries on
talking, threatening an invisible* LA CHUNGA.)
Now, you dike, you? Afraid, aren't you? Pissing yourself
with fear, aren't you? Now you're going to see how I deal
with insubordinate women. There's nothing I like more
than a woman who gets fresh with me. It makes me feel
randy if you want to know. Down on your knees. Bloody
hell, will you do as I say – if you don't want me to play
noughts and crosses all over your face. On your knees, I
said. You believe you're quite something, don't you? Just
because you've got this filthy pigsty – just because you've

saved the odd buck by exploiting bastards like us who come and drink your beer, and put up with your bad temper. Do you think I don't know who you are? Do you think all Piura doesn't know you were born in the Casa Verde, for Christ's sake. Amongst the prostitutes, the douches and the filth. Keep still there, I didn't tell you to get up, stay on your knees or I'll cut you to shreds, you bitch. Because that's what you are, Chunga. You were born in the Casa Verde, that's to say you're the daughter of a prostitute. So don't come the high and mighty with me, I know very well where you were dragged up. Now suck. Suck or I'll kill you, you bitch. Obey your man, and suck. Slowly and with feeling. Learn how to be my whore.

(*For a while, he mimes the scene, sweating, trembling, caressing the invisible* LA CHUNGA.)

Now swallow what you've got in your mouth. It's my birthday present. (*Lets out a little laugh, appeased and even a little bored*.) They say it's good for the complexion, ha ha. Did you get a fright? Did you think I was going to kill you? What a fool you are. I'm not capable of killing a woman. I'm really a gentleman, Chunguita. I respect the weaker sex. It's a game, you see? It excites me and I like it. Don't you have your little games too? When we know each other a little better you can tell me, and I'll oblige . . . I'm not one of those men who believe a woman shouldn't have her pleasure and that if you teach her to let herself go, she'll end up by being unfaithful to you. That's what José and Mono think. But not me, I'm fair-minded. Women have their rights too, why shouldn't they? Let's be friends, Chunguita, shall we? Don't be bitter. Let's make it up. Let's shake on it.

(LA CHUNGA *has materialized again beside* JOSEFINO.)

Now what do you say if we strike that bargain? We'll get rich, I swear.

LA CHUNGA: We wouldn't get rich. Perhaps we'd make more than I earn at the moment. But I'd certainly end up losing sooner or later. You'd make me feel that you were the stronger, like you're doing now. And if I ever disagreed

with you, out would come your knife, your fists, your
boots – you'd end up winning. I prefer to die poor than
to get rich with you.

JOSEFINO: (*Going to join the other superstuds, who are gambling
at the table*) How stupid women can be, God
Almighty . . .

The end of the party

Long pause between MECHE *and* LA CHUNGA *while they watch*
JOSEFINO *going down the staircase and taking up his seat again.*

MECHE: Chunga, can I go now? It'll soon be light. It must be
about six, mustn't it?

LA CHUNGA: Yes, you can go. Don't you want to sleep a little
first?

MECHE: If you don't mind, I'd prefer to go.

LA CHUNGA: I don't mind.
(*They go down the staircase together and head towards the exit.
They stop by the rocking chair. The superstuds have finished
their beers. They yawn as they play and appear not to see the
two women.*)

MECHE: (*A little hesitant*) If you want me to come back again,
and stay with you sometime, I mean at night . . .

LA CHUNGA: Of course I'd like us to spend another night
together.

MECHE: Right, there's no problem. I don't mind, Chunga, I
even . . .

LA CHUNGA: Wait, let me finish. I'd like to, but I don't want
to. I don't want you to spend another night with me, nor
do I want you ever to come back here.

MECHE: But why, Chunga? What have I done?

LA CHUNGA: (*Looking at her for a moment, silently, and then,
drawing her face towards her as before*) Because you are
very pretty. Because I like you and because you've made
me care about you, and what happens to you. That, for
me, is just as dangerous as falling in love, Meche. I told

215

you before I can't let myself be distracted. I'd lose the
battle. That's why I don't ever want to see you here again.

MECHE: I don't understand what you're saying, Chunga.

LA CHUNGA: I know you don't understand. It doesn't matter.

MECHE: Are you annoyed with me about something?

LA CHUNGA: No, I'm not annoyed about anything. (*Hands her
some money.*) Here. It's a present. For you, not for
Josefino. Don't let him have it, and don't tell him I gave
it to you.

MECHE: (*Confused*) No, I won't tell him anything. (*Hides the
money in her clothes.*) I feel ashamed to take money from
you. It makes me feel . . .

LA CHUNGA: A whore? You may as well get used to the idea,
in case you ever work in the Casa Verde. However . . .
Do you know what you're going to do with your life?
(MECHE *is about to answer but* LA CHUNGA *stops her.*)
Don't tell me. I don't want to know. If you leave Piura,
or stay, it's your affair. Don't tell me. Tonight I wanted
to help you, but tomorrow everything will be different.
You won't be here and everything will have changed. If
you do go, and you tell me where you're going, and Josefino
holds a knife to my throat, I'll end up by telling him
everything. I told you I didn't want to lose the battle. And
if they kill me, there'll be no more battle to lose. So come
on, make a decision and do what you think best. But above
all if you leave Piura, never even for a moment consider
telling me or writing to me or letting me know where you
are. OK?

MECHE: Right, Chunga. *Ciao*, then.

LA CHUNGA: *Ciao*, Meche. Good luck.
(MECHE *leaves the house.* LA CHUNGA *goes back to sit down
on her rocking chair. She remains in the same position she
was in when the curtain went up, at the beginning of the play.
The superstuds' voices are heard, beneath the smoke of the
cigars. Long pause.*)

LA CHUNGA: (*Energetically*) Time! Pay up and be off. I'm
closing.

EL MONO: Just five more minutes, Chunga.

LA CHUNGA: Not a second more, I said. Now, be off with the
lot of you. I'm tired.

LITUMA: (*Getting up*) I'm sleepy too. Besides, they've
completely cleaned me out, down to the very last copper.

JOSE: Yes, let's go – the night's become very flat all of a sudden.

EL MONO: But first let's sing the farewell song, superstuds.

(*They sing – their voices sound flat, as at the end of a party*)
We are the superstuds.
We don't want to work.
All we need is a little bit of skirt.
Drinking, gambling, all night long,
In Chunga's bar where we belong.
Wine, women and song –
Wine, women and song.
And now it's time to say 'so long'
Goodbye, Chunguita.

(*They get up, make their way towards the rocking chair.* LA
CHUNGA *gets up to take the money for the beers. They give
it to her between them.* LA CHUNGA *goes with them as far as
the door.*)

JOSE: (*Before crossing the threshhold, as if repeating a ritual*)
Tomorrow you'll tell me what happened that time with
Mechita, Chunga?

LA CHUNGA: (*Closing the door in his face*) Go and ask your
bloody mother. She'll tell you.

(*Outside, the superstuds laugh and sing rude songs.* LA
CHUNGA *bolts the door. She goes to put out the kerosene lamp
which hangs over the table where the superstuds gamble.
Sleepily she goes up to her room. It's clear from the way she
moves she is very tired. She lets herself fall on to the bed,
hardly taking off her sandals.*)

LA CHUNGA'S VOICE: Goodnight, Mechita. See you.